GYPSY TESTED RECIPES

BOBBIE ALTSCHUL

Copyright © 2013
Bobbie Altschul
All rights reserved.
ISBN-13: 978-1494802851
ISBN-10: 1494802856

DEDICATION

This book is dedicated to my husband and best friend, Hank. He suffered through several experiments from the kitchen which were less than successful. Needless to say, those recipes did not make their way into this book. Thank you, Honey. You tried them all and lived to tell about it!

I would also like to dedicate this book to my parents, Clyde and Marjorie Leininger, for all of their support and encouragement through the years. I love you both.

TABLE OF CONTENTS

	Acknowledgments	i
1	Appetizers	3
2	Salads and Soups	20
3	Breads and Rolls	38
4	Entrees	60
5	Side Dishes	87
6	Desserts	105
7	Beverages	127
8	Condiments	140
9	Misc.	153
10	Index	162
11	About the Author	170

ACKNOWLEDGMENTS

I have tried to acknowledge anyone who had a hand in the recipes that are in this publication. If I have forgotten anyone, please forgive me. It is very difficult to remember just where I got some of the better recipes since they have been in my kitchen for so very long.

Many of the recipes were found while we traveled from Michigan to Florida by the way of the river systems and some were found while traveling the United States in our motor home. Some have been handed down from friends and relatives!

They are all great!

APPETIZERS

Deviled Eggs

Ingredients:

12 eggs

Mayonnaise

Mustard yellow and brown spicy

Olives, black or green for garnish

Directions:

Boil eggs for 12 minutes. Cool and peel eggs. Cut eggs in half the long way.

Gently remove yolks and place into a bowl. Mash up the yolks well until crumbly. Add Mayonnaise and mustards. I usually use one large spoon of the Mayonnaise and then equal parts of the two mustards. Mix well until it is the consistency desired.

Fill the eggs back up with the mixture and place sliced olives on top.

Tangy Cheese Ball

This recipe comes from Bill Purkett in Havre, Montana. According to Bill the Tabasco sauce is the key ingredient.

Ingredients:

2 - 8 ounce packages cream cheese, room temperature

2 tablespoons dried green pepper flakes

½ cup sliced green olives with pimientos

½ cup diced black olives

1 tablespoon instant dried minced onions

2 Tabasco sauce

½ cup dried parsley flakes

Directions:

Blend cream cheese, green pepper flakes, olives onion, and Tabasco sauce with a fork in a medium-size bowl. Shape into a round ball. Roll in parsley flakes until covered slightly, pressing flakes against the ball as you roll it. Cover with plastic wrap and refrigerate for at least 1 hour before serving. Present on a platter surrounded with snack crackers.

This will keep in the refrigerator for up to 2 weeks.

Hot and Hearty Beef and Bean Dip

This recipe is from Betty Busse of Missoula, Montana.

Ingredients:

1 pound lean ground beef

1 – 2 ounce can green chilies

½ large onion, chopped

1 -16 ounce can refried beans

1 pound cheddar cheese, grated

4 ounces guacamole dip, mixed with

1 cup sour cream

Directions:

Brown ground beef in 12 inch skillet with chilies and onion. Drain fat. In an 8 x 10 baking pan, layer refried beans, ground beef and grated cheese. Bake 15 minutes at 350 degrees.

Remove from oven and spread the guacamole-sour cream mixture over top of ground beef mixture. Serve with Mexican style chips or crackers.

Nachos Supreme

This recipe was contributed by Gloria Loveday from Winnipeg.

Ingredients:

1 - 7 ½ ounce bag taco-flavored tortilla chips

1 ½ cups minced green pepper

1 ½ cups chopped tomatoes

1 ½ cups minced mushrooms

¾ cup minced onion

¾ cup minced celery

2 cups grated mild cheddar cheese

Directions:

Preheat broiler to 500 degrees.

Coat cookie sheet with non stick baking spray. Place layer of chips on cookie sheet; add layers of peppers, tomatoes and mushrooms. Mix celery and onion together and sprinkle over other ingredients. Cover with cheese. Place under broiler 3 to 5 minutes or until cheese has melted. Serve hot.

Fried Mozzarella-Pepperoni Egg Roll

Serves 6

Ingredients:

12 pieces of string cheese

12 egg roll wrappers

36 slices of pepperoni

Oil for deep-frying

Marinara or pizza sauce

Directions:

On top of an egg roll wrapper, place three pieces of pepperoni side by side in a row. Place a piece of string cheese on top. Fold corners over cheese. Fold bottom corner over cheese and pepperoni and keep rolling until cheese is tightly sealed. Moisten corners with water to seal. Repeat with the rest of wrappers, cheese and pepperoni.

In a skillet, heat oil to 375º F. Fry sticks, a few at a time, for 30-60 seconds on each side until completely brown. Drain on paper towels. Serve with sauce.

Hot Artichoke Spread

Ingredients:

1 cup Miracle Whip salad dressing

1 cup parmesan cheese

1 – 14 ounce can artichoke hearts, drained and chopped

1 – 14 ounce can chopped greed chilies, drained

1 clove garlic, minced

2 tablespoons green onion slices

2 tablespoons chopped tomatoes

Directions:

Preheat oven to 350 degrees. Mix together salad dressing, parmesan cheese, artichoke hearts, chopped chilies and garlic well until blended. Spoon into shallow oven proof dish or 9 inch pie plate. Bake 20 to 25 minutes or until lightly browned. Sprinkle with onion and tomato. Serve with Fritos, tortilla chips or crackers.

Beer-Cheese Triangles with Zesty Cheese Sauce

Ingredients:

2 cups Original Bisquick™ mix

1/2 cup shredded Cheddar cheese (2 oz)

1/2 cup beer or apple sauce

2 tablespoons butter or margarine, melted

1/4 cup sesame or poppy seed

1 loaf (8 oz) prepared cheese product, cut into cubes

1/4 cup Old El Paso™ Thick 'n Chunky salsa

1/4 cup Old El Paso™ refried beans

Directions:

Line cookie sheets with waxed paper. In medium bowl, stir Bisquick mix, Cheddar cheese and beer until soft dough forms; beat vigorously 20 strokes. On surface sprinkled with Bisquick mix, roll dough in Bisquick mix to coat. Shape into a ball; knead 5 times.

Press or roll dough into 16x10-inch rectangle. Cut rectangle into 2-inch squares (do not separate); cut squares diagonally in half. Spread with melted butter; sprinkle with sesame seed. Separate triangles and place on cookie sheet. Freeze until firm, about 1 hour. Place frozen triangles in airtight container. Freeze up to 1 month.

Heat oven to 450°F. Spray large cookie sheets with cooking spray. Place triangles on cookie sheets. Bake 8 to 10 minutes or until golden brown.

To make sauce, in 1 1/2-quart saucepan, heat cheese product, salsa and beans over low heat, stirring occasionally, until cheese is melted and sauce is hot. Serve triangles with sauce.

Almost-Famous Spinach-Artichoke Dip

Ingredients:

Kosher salt
2 10-ounce bags spinach, stems removed
1 tablespoons unsalted butter
2 tablespoons minced onion
1 clove garlic, minced
2 teaspoons all-purpose flour
1 1/4 cups whole milk
1/2 teaspoon fresh lemon juice
1 teaspoon Worcestershire sauce
1 1/4 cup
1/4 cup sour cream, plus more for serving
1/2 cup frozen artichoke hearts, thawed, squeezed dry and roughly chopped
Tortilla chips and salsa, for serving

Directions:

Bring a large pot of salted water to a boil. Stir in the spinach and cook until bright green, about 30 seconds. Drain and rinse under cold water; squeeze out the excess moisture, then finely chop.

Melt the butter in a large saucepan over medium heat. Add the onion, garlic and 1/2 teaspoon salt and cook until the onion is soft, about 2 minutes. Add the flour and cook, stirring, until lightly toasted, about 1 minute. Whisk in the milk and cook, whisking constantly, until thickened, about 1 minute. Remove from the heat. Stir in the lemon juice, Worcestershire sauce, parmesan and sour cream.

Return the pot to medium heat. Add the spinach, cheddar and artichokes and stir until the cheese melts and the dip is heated through. Serve warm with tortilla chips, salsa and sour cream.

Crisp Crab Cakes

Yield: 8 crab cakes

Ingredients:

12 scallions, thinly sliced
1/2 cup finely chopped red bell pepper
1 cup panko (Japanese breadcrumbs)
1 large egg, lightly beaten
2 tablespoons nonfat milk
1 teaspoon Worcestershire sauce
2 teaspoons Dijon mustard
1 tablespoon fresh lemon juice, plus lemon wedges for serving
1/2 teaspoon Old Bay Seasoning
Dash of hot sauce
1 pound lump crab or crab claw meat, picked over
Kosher salt and freshly ground pepper
Olive-oil cooking spray

Directions:

Heat 2 teaspoons olive oil in a large nonstick skillet over medium-high heat. Add the scallions and bell pepper and cook until they begin to soften, about 2 minutes. Cool slightly.

Mix 1/2 cup panko, the egg and milk in a small bowl. In a medium bowl, whisk the Worcestershire sauce, mustard, lemon juice, Old Bay and hot sauce; fold in the crabmeat, panko mixture, scallion, bell pepper mixture, 1/4 teaspoon salt and a pinch of pepper. Shape into 8 patties and refrigerate 30 minutes.

Coat the crab cakes with the remaining 1/2 cup panko. Heat the remaining 1 tablespoon olive oil in the skillet over medium-high heat. Mist the crab cakes with cooking spray and cook, sprayed-side down, 3 to 4 minutes. Spray the tops, flip and cook 3 to 4 more minutes. Serve with lemon wedges.

Hot Crab Dip

Ingredients:

8 ounces reduced-fat cream cheese (Neufchatel), room temperature

1/4 cup reduced-fat sour cream

1/4 teaspoon hot sauce

1/4 teaspoon crab boil spices, (recommended: Old Bay)

1 garlic clove, minced

Kosher salt and freshly ground pepper

12 ounces fresh crab meat, picked over for bits of shell and patted dry

2 scallions, thinly sliced

2 tablespoons chopped fresh parsley

2 to 3 teaspoons fresh lemon juice

Whole-wheat crackers for serving, optional

Directions:

Stir together the cream cheese, sour cream, hot sauce, crab boil spice, and garlic in a medium saucepan until smooth; season, to taste, with salt and pepper. Heat the cream cheese mixture over medium-low heat until warm, stirring constantly, 2 to 3 minutes. Fold in the crab, scallions, parsley and lemon juice and warm until heated through, about 1 minute more. Serve immediately.

Reduced fat cream cheese and sour cream are the healthy key to this creamy dip. A bit of crab boil spice, hot sauce, lemon and herbs keep it fresh tasting.

Five Layer Mexican Dip

Ingredients:

2 teaspoons olive oil

1 medium onion, diced

2 cloves garlic, minced

1 (15.5-ounce) can black beans, preferably low-sodium, drained and rinsed

1 tablespoon minced chipotle pepper in adobo

4 tablespoons lime juice

1/4 teaspoon ground cumin

1 tablespoon water

1/2 teaspoon salt

2 cups corn kernels (10-ounce box frozen corn)

1/4 cup chopped cilantro leaves

2 ripe avocados

4 medium tomatoes, seeded and diced (about 2 cups)

1/4 cup thinly sliced scallion

1 tablespoon finely diced jalapeno pepper, optional

3/4 cup shredded extra-sharp Cheddar

Directions:

Heat the oil in a skillet over medium-high heat. Add onions and cook until they soften, about 3 minutes. Stir in the garlic and cook for 2 minutes more.

Put half of the onion mixture into a food processor with the black beans, chipotle pepper, 2 tablespoons of the lime juice, cumin, water and salt. Puree until smooth. Set aside.

Add the corn to the skillet with the remaining onion mixture and cook for about 3 minutes. Remove from the heat and stir in the cilantro leaves.

In a small bowl mash the avocado with the remaining lime juice. In a medium bowl toss together the tomatoes, scallion and jalapeno, if using. Season tomato mixture with salt and pepper, to taste.

Spread the black bean dip into the bottom of an 8 by 8 glass baking or serving dish. Top with the corn mixture, spreading it out to form a single layer over the beans, repeat with the avocado, then the tomatoes. Top with cheese. Serve with baked chips.

Buttery Mushrooms

Ingredients:

2 pounds unsalted butter

2 tablespoons seasoning salt

2 tablespoons seasoning pepper

16 cloves of garlic

5 small packages of mushrooms or 3 large packages

Directions:

Melt butter in crock pot with seasonings and garlic (smash the cloves or chop them as desired) on high.

Start adding the cleaned mushrooms into the mixture stirring to cover. Cook on high for a couple of hours, pressing down the mushrooms and adding more as the liquid allows until all of the mushrooms are in the crock pot. (All of the mushrooms won't normally fit all at once.)

Turn down to low and cook for another two hours at least, stirring occasionally.

Serve hot.

This is a recipe that my friend, Nancy Curnick made while we were boating together. They were so good I have taken them to pot lucks all around the country. The recipe was requested so often that anytime I take them somewhere, I print off several copies to hand out.

Crab Rangoon Dip

Ingredients:

2 cups crab meat

16 oz. cream cheese (2 blocks)

1/2 cup sour cream

4 green onions, chopped

1 1/2 tsp. Worcestershire sauce

2 Tbsp powdered sugar

1/2 tsp garlic powder

1/2 tsp lemon juice

Directions:

First, soften the cream cheese in the microwave for about a minute.

Chop your green onions. Add them and your two cups of crab meat.

Add the sour cream, Worcestershire sauce, powdered sugar, garlic powder and lemon juice.

Mix all the ingredients and bake for 30 minutes at 350 degrees.

Serve hot with chips or fried wontons or pork rinds.

Louisiana Hot Crap Dip

Ingredients:

1/2 pound jumbo lump crabmeat, free of shells

1 (8 ounce) package cream cheese

1/2 cup mayonnaise

1/4 cup grated Parmesan

3 tablespoons minced green onions (white and green parts)

2 large garlic cloves, minced

2 teaspoons Worcestershire sauce

2 tablespoons fresh lemon juice

1 teaspoon hot sauce

1/2 teaspoon Old Bay seasoning

Salt and pepper to taste

Directions:

Preheat oven to 325 degrees F. Combine all of the ingredients in a casserole dish and gently stir until thoroughly mixed. Adjust seasoning to taste. Bake for 35 to 40 minutes until lightly golden on top. Serve hot, with hot sauce on the side for those who like it spicy. Makes about 1 1/2 cups

Hot Cheesy Artichoke & Spinach Dip

Frisky Three cheeses bring their distinctive flavors to this rich, delicious hot artichoke dip.

Ingredients:

1 (14 ounce) can artichoke hearts, drained

1/3 cup grated Romano cheese

1/4 cup grated Parmesan cheese

1/2 teaspoon minced garlic

1 (10 ounce) package frozen chopped spinach, thawed and drained
1/3 cup heavy cream

1/2 cup sour cream

1 cup shredded mozzarella cheese

Directions:

Preheat oven to 350 degrees F (175 degrees C). Grease a 9x13 inch baking dish.

In a blender or food processor, place artichoke hearts, Romano cheese, Parmesan cheese and garlic. Pulse until chopped, but not ground. Set aside.

In a medium bowl, mix together spinach, heavy cream, sour cream and mozzarella cheese. Stir in artichoke mixture. Spoon into prepared baking dish.

Bake in the preheated oven for 20 to 25 minutes, or until cheese is melted and bubbly.

SALADS AND SOUPS

Bobbie's Chili

Ingredients:

1 pound lean ground beef or chuck
1 package of dry onion soup
2 small cans tomato soup
2 cans kidney beans
¼ cup dry parsley
1 teaspoon oregano
2 tablespoons chili powder

Toppings:

Diced onions
Shredded cheddar cheese
Frito corn chips

Directions:

Brown meat with the dry onion soup until meat is cooked through, this can be put into a crock pot or big pot on the stove.

Add the tomato soup along with a soup can of water for each can, kidney beans (no need to drain and rinse), parsley, oregano and chili powder.

Simmer on stove stirring often for a couple of hours. In the crock pot I leave it on high for four hours and then turn it down on low with the lid off for another half hour.

Serve with fresh, diced onions; grated cheddar cheese and Frito corn chips.

Chili is even better heated up on the second day!

White Chili

Ingredients:

4 chicken breasts
1 – 48 ounce jar Northern beans
1 – 24 ounce jar salsa
1 cup shredded cheese

Directions:

Put thawed breasts at bottom of crock pot. Cover with jar of beans and jar of salsa. Cook on high 6 to 8 hours.

Remove chicken from the mixture and shred it and return it to the pot. I add water if the chili is too thick.

We like this chili with corn bread instead of crackers but crackers work well also.

Before serving, add cheese.

Quick Crab Stew

Ingredients:

2 tablespoons butter

1 small onion, chopped

1 (10 3/4-ounce) can condensed cream of potato soup

1 (10 3/4-ounce) can condensed cream of celery soup

1 soup can milk

1 soup can half-and-half

1 pound claw crabmeat, picked free of any broken shells

1/4 cup dry sherry

Salt and freshly ground black pepper

Directions:

In a large saucepan, melt the butter and sauté the onion until translucent, 3 to 4 minutes. Add the soups, milk, and half-and-half. Add the crabmeat and bring just to a boil. Add the sherry and salt and pepper, to taste. Serve immediately. Or allow to cool to room temperature, then refrigerate or freeze immediately in plastic microwavable reusable containers with lids.

Egg Drop Soup

Ingredients:

2 cups water

2 chicken bouillon cubes

1 scallion with green top

2 eggs, beaten

Directions:

Bring water and bouillon cubes to a rolling boil. Chop scallion finely and add to the water mixture. Add eggs while stirring vigorously with a fork. Reduce heat and simmer for 3 minutes.

Makes 2 – 1 cup servings.

Potato Soup

Ingredients:

3 cups potatoes, diced

2 cups water

½ cup celery, cut fine

½ cup carrots, diced

½ cup onion, diced

1 teaspoon parsley flakes

2 chicken bouillon cubes

½ teaspoon salt

1 package ham, diced

2 cups milk

2 tablespoons flour

4 cheese slices

3 tablespoons butter

Directions:

Cook together potatoes, water, celery, carrots, onion, parsley flakes, bouillon cubes and salt until tender. Then add ham pieces. In a small pan add 2 cups milk, 3 tablespoons butter and cheese slices.

Heat together on medium than take a small bowl and add 2 tablespoons flour and add a little hot water to flour and make a paste. Then add mixture to milk, butter etc. mixture, stir with whisk until slightly thick. Pour over vegetable mixture and it's ready to eat.

Broccoli Salad

This recipe is from Marie Mickey from Lompoc, California. As a matter of fact, her nutritious salad was a winner at the Nevada State Cook-Off. Water chestnuts give it extra crunch.

Ingredients:

2 large bunches broccoli, finely chopped

1 large red onion, finely chopped

8 celery stalks, finely chopped

1 – 8 ounce can water chestnuts, finely chopped

1 – 4 ounce can chopped black olives

2 tablespoons oregano

Cherry tomatoes (optional)

1 – 16 ounce Italian dressing (Marie prefers Kraft)

Directions:

Mix all ingredients in a large bowl until well blended. Allow to stand for 2 hours until flavors mellow. Salad can be kept in refrigerator for several days.

I add ½ cup sugar when mixing. That seems to take some of the tartness out of the Italian dressing. Also, when serving I add a little shredded cheddar cheese on top.

Tex-Mex Salad

Ingredients:

½ cup sour cream

1 – 2 tablespoons lime juice

½ teaspoon sugar

½ teaspoon kosher salt

½ head shredded lettuce

½ cup plum tomato, chopped

½ cup cilantro, chopped

½ cup scallion, chopped

½ cup cheddar cheese, shredded

Directions:

Wisk sour cream, lime juice, sugar and salt together in a large bowl. Toss with lettuce, tomato, cilantro, scallion and cheese.

Spanish Potato Salad

Ingredients:

1 ½ pounds red-skinned potatoes, quartered

¾ cup pimientos

¾ cup celery

¾ cup green olives

2 tablespoons parsley, chopped

2 tablespoons sherry vinegar

2 tablespoons mayonnaise

1 tablespoon olive oil

1 tablespoon shallot, chopped

¼ teaspoon smoked paprika

Directions:

Cook potatoes in simmering salted water until tender, about 10 to 15 minutes. Drain; cool slightly. Combine all other ingredients.

Toss with the potatoes and season with salt and pepper to taste.

Cool Whip Salad

Ingredients:

1 – 9 ounce carton Cool Whip

1 – 3 ounce package pistachio pudding, instant

1 cup mini-marshmallows

1 large can crushed pineapple with juice

1 11- ounce can mandarin oranges, drained

Directions:

Mix Cool Whip, pudding, marshmallows, pineapple, and oranges together. Chill

Oriental Slaw

Ingredients:

1 bag shredded cabbage slaw

6-8 green onions, chopped

2 bags slivered almonds

2 packages Ramen noodles, do not use flavor packet

1 cup peanut oil

1 cup sugar

½ cup white cider vinegar

3 tablespoons sesame seeds

4 tablespoons oleo

½ teaspoon pepper

2 tablespoons soy sauce

Directions:

In large salad bowl combine cabbage slaw, onions, almonds and sesame seeds.

Crush and brown Ramen noodles in oleo in fry pan.

Whisk oil, sugar, vinegar, pepper and soy sauce until blended.

Mix dressing with the slaw just before serving.

Crab Pasta Salad

Helen Kost from Rogue River, Oregon is the writer of this recipe and she says it can be served as a main course as well as a salad.

Ingredients:

4 cups water
1 teaspoon salt
1 teaspoon cooking oil
2 cups curly noodles, uncooked
¾ cup crabmeat, chopped
3 green onions, diced, including some of the tops
1 large stalk celery, diced
¼ cup sliced black olives
1/3 cup mayonnaise
¼ cup half and half or milk
Salt and pepper to taste
1 egg, hard boiled, sliced
½ large tomato, sliced or cut in chunks

Directions:

In a 4 quart kettle, bring water, salt and cooking oil to boil. Add noodles and cook 10 minutes. Drain in colander, rinse under cold water and transfer to a bowl.

Add crabmeat, onions, celery and olives and mix well.

In a small bowl, mix mayonnaise, half and half, salt and pepper. Add dressing to salad and toss lightly. Refrigerate until ready to serve. Decorate with sliced egg and tomato pieces.

Chilistroni

This recipe is from Ilene Norton in Springfield, Oregon.

Ingredients:

½ pound ground beef

3 cloves garlic, minced

½ cup chopped onion

½ cup sliced celery

1 – 28 ounce can tomatoes, cut into small pieces

1 - 10 ¾ ounce can beef broth

1 soup can water

2 teaspoons chili powder

1 – 15 ¼ ounce can kidney beans, undrained

2 medium zucchini, sliced

3 cups frozen mixed vegetables

Salt and pepper to taste

2 cups cooked macaroni

Directions:

In a Dutch oven, brown beef, draining off fat, add garlic and onion and sauté 1 minute. Add remaining ingredients, except macaroni. Cover and simmer 25 minutes. Add macaroni and simmer a few more minutes. If too thick, add a little more water to the soup.

I have made this in the crock pot and let it all simmer several hours while we traveled and added the macaroni the last half hour.

Cucumber Salad in a Jar

Ingredients:

4 thinly sliced cucumbers

1-large sliced red onions

1-large sliced green bell peppers

1-tbsp salt

2-cup white vinegar

1 1/2-cups sugar

1-tsp celery flakes

1-tsp red pepper flakes

Directions:

Put vinegar, sugar, celery flakes and pepper flakes in a pot and bring to a boil. Remove from heat and add 2 handfuls of ice until melted.

Place all veggies in large mouth canning jars (2 quarts or 1 half gallon jar)

Pour mixture over cucumbers, store in refrigerator.

Will keep up to 2 months (Makes 2 quart jars)

Best Ever Coleslaw

Shredded cabbage as desired.

Add Briannas Home Style Poppy Seed Dressing to desired consistency.

Chill and serve.

Note: Probably any white poppy seed dressing would work but I have found this to be the best.

I have had raves about this simple recipe. Even from folks that say they don't like coleslaw!!

Healthy Shrimp Salad

The shrimp for this salad could be boiled or sautéed.

Ingredients:

1 pound large, peeled shrimp

2-3 red ripe tomatoes

6 fresh okra, split in half (or substitute snow peas, my favorite)

½ cup red onion

1 large cucumber

Olive oil

Rice vinegar

Salt and pepper

Directions:

Season the shrimp and sauté quickly in a little hot oil, then set aside to cool.

Dice the tomatoes, season to your taste with salt and pepper and place in a large salad bowl.

Chop the red onion into interesting shapes and add to the tomatoes. Slice the cucumber and add as well.

Season okra or snow peas and brown until brown and add to the salad.

Mix equal parts of the vinegar and oil until blended well and add to the salad. Give the salad a good toss and serve chilled.

Creamy Avocado Pasta Salad

Ingredients:

2 avocados, pitted

1 lemon juiced

Lemon zest

2 garlic cloves

1 teaspoon kosher salt

2 tablespoons olive oil

16 oz pasta

Tomatoes

Directions:

Boil pasta and cook until Al Dente.

Put remaining ingredients (except lemon zest) into a food processor and process until smooth and creamy.

Drain pasta and combine with sauce. Top with tomatoes and zest.

Shrimp and Pineapple Lettuce Cups

Ingredients:

1 pound fresh peeled, deveined cooked shrimp

1 ½ cups chopped fresh pineapple

1 cup chopped red sweet pepper

½ cup snipped fresh cilantro

2 teaspoons toasted sesame oil

1 head Bibb lettuce, leaves separated

Directions:

Coarsely chop shrimp. In a medium bowl stir together shrimp, pineapple, sweet pepper, cilantro and sesame oil. Season to taste with salt and black pepper.

To serve, spoon shrimp mixture into lettuce leaves.

Crockpot French Onion Soup

Ingredients:

3 large onions, sliced (3 cups)
3 tablespoons margarine or butter, melted
3 tablespoons all-purpose flour
1 tablespoon Worcestershire sauce
1 teaspoon sugar
1/4 teaspoon pepper
4 cans (14 1/2 ounces each) ready-to-serve beef broth

Cheesy Broiled French bread:

8 slices French bread, 1 inch thick
3/4 cup shredded mozzarella cheese (3 ounces)
2 tablespoons grated or shredded Parmesan cheese

Directions:

In lined slow cooker, mix onions and margarine.

Cover and cook on high heat setting 30 to 35 minutes or until onions begin to slightly brown around edges.

Mix flour, Worcestershire sauce, sugar and pepper. Stir flour mixture and broth into onions. Cover and cook on low heat setting 7 to 9 hours (or high heat setting 3 to 4 hours) or until onions are very tender.

Prepare Cheesy Broiled French Bread, broiling until bubbly. Place 1 slice bread on top of each bowl of soup.

BREADS AND ROLLS

Muffins That Taste Like Donuts

(But without all the work and without the frying)! Now who doesn't love that???

Ingredients:

3/4 cup sugar

1 large egg

1 1/2 cups all-purpose flour

2 teaspoon baking power

1/4 teaspoon salt

1/4 teaspoon ground nutmeg

1/4 cup vegetable oil

3/4 cup milk

1 teaspoon vanilla extract

2 tablespoon butter, melted

1/2 cup sugar, for rolling (I added in a few shakes of cinnamon)

Preheat oven to 350. Lightly grease a muffin tin. In a large bowl, beat together sugar and egg until light in color. In a small bowl, whisk together flour, baking powder, salt and nutmeg. Pour into egg mixture and stir to combine. Pour in vegetable oil, milk and vanilla extract. Divide batter evenly into 10 muffin cups, filling each about 3/4 full. Bake for 15-18 minutes, until a tester inserted into the center comes out clean.

While muffins are baking, melt butter and pour remaining sugar into a small bowl. When muffins are done, lightly brush the top of each with some melted butter, remove from the pan and roll in sugar. Cool on a wire rack.

Yeast-Free Bread

Carbonation from your favorite soda pop or seltzer stimulates the leavening in the self-rising flour for this mighty-quick bread.

Ingredients:

2 1/2 cups self-rising flour

3 tablespoons white sugar

1 (12 fluid ounce) can or bottle lemon-lime flavored carbonated beverage

Directions:

Preheat oven to 350 degrees F (175 degrees C). Grease one 9×5 inch loaf pan.

Combine the flour, sugar and carbonated beverage. Mix well and place into the prepared pan.

Bake at 350 degrees F (175 degrees C) for 45 minutes. Note: If using a sweetened carbonated beverage cut back on the sugar a little.

Simple Flat Bread

Ingredients:

1 package active yeast

1/2 teaspoon sugar

1 cup all-purpose flour

3/4 cup whole wheat flour

1 teaspoon coarse salt

2 teaspoons Italian seasoning

3/4 cup water

Oil

Directions:

In the bowl of your food processor, pulse together yeast, sugar, flour, salt, and Italian seasoning.

Slowly pour in the water (you may need a little more than 3/4 cup). Mix until the dough forms into a ball. This takes a few minutes.

Remove the dough from the bowl and knead it for a few minutes until the dough is smooth.

Use a bit of oil to coat a large bowl. Place the dough in the greased bowl, cover with a damp towel, and allow to rise for one hour.

After the dough has doubled in size, punch it down, and knead for a few minutes.

Divide the dough into 6 equal pieces, and roll each piece into a 7-8 inch circle.

Heat a non-stick skillet to medium heat. You do NOT need to grease the pan. When it's warm, cook one piece of flat bread at a time for about 1-2 to minutes per side. When the bread starts to brown, you know it's done.

This bread can be stored in an air-tight container for a few days, but it's best eaten within a day or two.

Surprise Muffins

Ingredients:

1 egg, beaten with fork

1 c. milk

2 c. sifted flour

1/4 c. melted shortening

3 tsp. baking powder

1/2 tsp. salt

2 tbsp. sugar

Preserves, your choice

Directions:

Sift flour, baking powder, salt and sugar.

Thoroughly mix milk, melted shortening and egg together.

Pour liquid mixture into flour mixture, stirring lightly until flour mixture is just moist.

Fill greased and floured muffin cups or paper liners about 1/3 full. Carefully center 2 teaspoons of preserves over batter and cover with enough batter to fill muffin cups 2/3 full. Bake at 425° for 20 to 25 minutes.

Griddle Flat Bread

Ingredients:

3 cups all purpose flour

1 cup ice water

3 tablespoons shortening

2 teaspoons salt

2 teaspoons baking powder

Pinch of baking soda

Directions:

Combine all ingredients and form into a dough. Cut into 4 or 5 equal pieces. Roll out to a thin 8 inch circle. Prick the surface of the dough with a fork and cook on an oiled hot griddle. Turn with a spatula. Watch these flat bread disks closely because they cook fast. Serve warm.

Red Lobster Cheese Biscuits

This recipe was given to us by Greg who was a pressman working for us when we had a commercial print shop. He worked at a Red Lobster for a time.

Ingredients:

2 cups Bisquick mix

2/3 cup milk

½ cup shredded cheese

¼ cup melted butter

¼ cup garlic powder

Directions:

Mix Bisquick, milk and cheese. Beat for about 30 seconds. Drop by teaspoonful onto cookie sheet. Bake at 50 degrees until brown. Mix butter and garlic powder together and brush over biscuits.

Poppy Seed Bread

Ingredients:

1 box yellow cake mix

3 eggs

½ cup oil

1 cup hot water

1 (3 ounce) vanilla or coconut instant pudding

2 tablespoons poppy seeds

Directions:

Mix cake mix, eggs, oil, water, pudding and poppy seeds together. Pour into 2 greased and floured loaf pans. Bake at 350 degrees for 35 to 40 minutes.

Buttery Soft Pretzels

Ingredients:

4 teaspoons active dry yeast

1 teaspoon white sugar

1 1/4 cups warm water (110 degrees F/45 degrees C)

5 cups all-purpose flour

1/2 cup white sugar

1 1/2 teaspoons salt

1 tablespoon vegetable oil

1/2 cup baking soda

4 cups hot water

1/4 cup kosher salt, for topping

Directions:

In a small bowl, dissolve yeast and 1 teaspoon sugar in 1 1/4 cup warm water. Let stand until creamy, about 10 minutes.

In a large bowl, mix together flour, 1/2 cup sugar, and salt. Make a well in the center; add the oil and yeast mixture. Mix and form into a dough. If the mixture is dry, add one or two more tablespoons of water. Knead the dough until smooth, about 7 to 8 minutes. Lightly oil a large bowl, place the dough in the bowl, and turn to coat with oil. Cover with plastic wrap and let rise in a warm place until doubled in size, about 1 hour.

Preheat oven to 450 degrees F (230 degrees C). Grease 2 baking sheets.

In a large bowl, dissolve baking soda in 4 cups hot water; set aside. When risen, turn dough out onto a lightly floured surface and divide into 12 equal pieces. Roll each piece into a rope and twist into a pretzel shape. Once all of the dough is shaped, dip each pretzel into the baking soda-hot water solution and place pretzels on baking sheets. Sprinkle with kosher salt.

Bake in preheated oven until browned, about 8 minutes.

Homemade Pan Rolls

Ingredients:

2 1/2 to 3 cups Gold Medal™ all-purpose flour

1/4 cup sugar

1/4 cup shortening

1 teaspoon salt

1 package regular or quick active dry yeast

1/2 cup very warm water (120°F to 130°F)

1/2 cup very warm milk (120°F to 130°F)

1 egg

Butter or margarine, melted

Directions:

Mix 2 cups of the flour, the sugar, shortening, salt and yeast in medium bowl. Add warm water, warm milk and egg. Beat with electric mixer on low speed 1 minute, scraping bowl frequently. Beat on medium speed 1 minute, scraping bowl frequently. Stir in enough remaining flour to make dough easy to handle.

Turn dough onto lightly floured surface. Knead about 5 minutes or until smooth and elastic. Place in greased bowl and turn greased side up. Cover and let rise in warm place about 1 hour or until double. Dough is ready if indentation remains when touched.

Grease bottoms and sides of 2 round pans, 9x1 1/2 inches.

Punch down dough. Cut dough in half; cut each half into 24 pieces. Shape into balls. Place close together in pans. Brush with butter. Cover and let rise in warm place about 30 minutes or until double.

Heat oven to 400°F.

Bake 12 to 18 minutes or until golden brown.

Beer Bread

Ingredients:

3 cups flour (sifted)

3 teaspoons baking powder (omit if using Self-Rising Flour)

1 teaspoon salt (omit if using Self-Rising Flour)

1/4 cup sugar

1 (12 ounce) can beer

1/2 cup melted butter

Directions:

Preheat oven to 350 degrees

Mix dry ingredients and beer.

Pour into a greased loaf pan.

Pour melted butter over mixture.

Bake 1 hour, remove from pan and cool for at least 15 minutes.

This recipe makes a very hearty bread with a crunchy, buttery crust. If you prefer a softer crust (like a traditional bread) mix the butter into the batter instead of pouring it over the top.

Banana Bread #1

There are a lot of banana bread recipes. I have put two in this book. Of the two, I think this is the easiest.

Ingredients:

¾ cup margarine

1 ½ cup sugar

4 eggs

5 bananas, mashed

3 cups flour

1 ½ teaspoon baking soda

1 ½ teaspoon salt

1 ½ teaspoon vanilla

¾ cup nuts, chopped (optional)

Directions:

Preheat oven to 350 degrees. Grease 2 loaf pans. Cream margarine and sugar. Add eggs and bananas. Sift together flour, soda and salt. Add sifted ingredients, mixing well. Mix in vanilla and nuts. Pour into bans. Bake 60 to 75 minutes. Cool 10 minutes; remove from pans.

Monkey Bread

There are all sorts of recipes for monkey bread out there but I find this is the easiest.

Ingredients:

2 packages refrigerated biscuits in tube

¼ cup sugar

¼ cup cinnamon

Directions:

Cut biscuits into quarters. Place in Ziploc bag with sugar and cinnamon and shake.

Place biscuit quarters in a greased pan and bake at 350 degrees for 30 minutes. Let stand 5 minutes after removing from pan. Serve on a plate. Pull apart with forks.

Southern Biscuits

Ingredients:

3 ½ cups all-purpose flour (preferably soft wheat like Martha White or White Lily)

1 ½ tablespoons baking powder

¾ teaspoon baking soda

1 ½ tablespoon sugar

¾ teaspoon salt

6 tablespoons butter, cut up and cold

2 cups buttermilk, cold

2 tablespoon melted butter

Directions:

Preheat oven to 500 degrees. Grease 9 inch square baking pan and 1/3 cup measuring cup. Sprinkle ½ cup flour on rimmed baking sheet.

In food processor, pulse 3 cups flour, baking powder, baking soda, sugar and salt; add butter. Pulse to form coarse crumbs; transfer to bowl.

With rubber spatula, stir buttermilk into flour mixture until just combined. With greased measuring cup, scoop 9 heaping cupfuls dough on floured baking sheet. Lightly dust tops of mounds with flour from sheet. With floured hands, gently arrange mounds in pan in 3 rows of 3.

Brush with melted butter. Bake 5 minutes. Reset oven to 450 degrees. Bake 15 to 20 minutes or until golden.

Basic Bread for Beginners

This is the easiest one-loaf yeast bread you will ever bake. The Super Easy Bread for Beginners recipe produces a soft crust and a moist center using the most basic ingredients that can be found in most kitchens.

Ingredients:

3/4 cup warm water

1 package active dry yeast

1 tsp salt

1-1/2 tbsp sugar

1 tbsp vegetable shortening

1/2 cup milk

3 cups all-purpose flour, approximately

Directions:

In large bowl, add the warm water. Slowly stir in dry yeast. Continue to stir until yeast is dissolved.

Add salt, sugar, shortening, and milk to bowl. Stir.

Mix in the first 2 cups of flour.

If needed, begin adding more flour, one tablespoon at a time, until the dough chases the spoon around the bowl.

You do not need to use up all the flour called for in this recipe, or you may need more flour than called for. The amounts vary depending on many factors, including weather, which is why most bread recipes only give an approximate amount of flour needed.

Turn dough out onto floured board and knead, adding small spoonfuls of flour as needed, until the dough is soft and smooth, not sticky to the touch.

Put dough in buttered bowl, turn dough over so that the top of dough is greased. Cover and let rise in warm spot for 1 hour.

Punch down dough. Turn out onto floured board and knead.

Preheat oven at 375 degrees F.

Form dough into loaf and set in buttered bread pan. Cover and let rise for about 30 minutes.

Score dough by cutting three slashes across the top with a sharp knife. Put in oven and bake for about 45 minutes or until golden brown.

Turn out bread and let cool on a rack or clean dishtowel.

Banana Bread #2

Ingredients:

3 very ripe bananas, peeled

1/3 cup melted butter

3/4 cup sugar (1/4 cup more if you like it very sweet, 1/4 cup less if you like it less sweet)

1 egg, beaten

1 teaspoon vanilla extract

1 teaspoon baking soda

Pinch of salt

1 1/2 cups of all-purpose flour

Directions:

Preheat the oven to 350°F (175°C), and butter a 4x8-inch loaf pan.

In a large mixing bowl, mash the ripe bananas with a fork. Use a wooden spoon to stir the melted butter into the mashed bananas.

Mix in the baking soda and salt. Stir in the sugar, beaten egg, and vanilla extract. Mix in the flour.

Pour the batter into your prepared loaf pan. Bake for 1 hour to 1 hour 10 minutes at 350°F (175°C), or until a tester inserted into the center comes out clean.

Remove from oven and cool completely on a rack. Remove the banana bread from the pan. Slice and serve. (A bread knife helps to make slices that aren't crumbly.)

ENTREES

White Chicken Enchiladas

Ingredients:

8 flour tortillas

2 cups cooked, shredded chicken

2 cups shredded Monterey Jack cheese

3 Tbsp butter

3 Tbsp flour

2 cups chicken broth

1 cup sour cream

1 (4 oz) can diced green chilies

Directions:

Preheat oven to 350 degrees.

Spray a 9x13 pan with cooking spray.

Mix chicken and 1 cup cheese.

Roll tortillas and place in pan seam side down.

In a sauce pan melt butter under low heat. Stir in flour and cook about 1 minute. Add broth and stir until smooth. Allow to thicken. Remove from heat and stir in sour cream and chilies.

Pour sauce over enchiladas and top with remaining cheese. Bake 20-25 minutes and then broil for a few minutes to brown the cheese.

Shrimp Boat Spaghetti

Ingredients:

1 pound pasta

1 pound large peeled shrimp

3-4 large, ripe tomatoes

1 green bell pepper

Red pepper flakes

Salt and pepper

Directions:

Cook pasta according to the package directions.

Season the shrimp and cook over high heat in a little oil. They should be done in 3 minutes if the pan is not overcrowded. Set aside to drain on paper towels.

Sauté the bell pepper in a little oil, add the garlic and a pinch or two of the red pepper flakes.

Cut the tomatoes into large cubes and add it as well. Cook 5 or 6 minutes. Add the shrimp, toss in the pasta and serve at once.

Serve with a crusty bread that will be ideal for sopping up the sauce.

Shrimp and Mango Stir-Fry

Ingredients:

¼ pound steamed or dry Chinese noodles

1 ripe mango, cubed (1 cup)

1 cup sliced onion

1 cup sliced red bell pepper

¼ pound fresh snow peas, trimmed (about 2 cups)

¼ cup cashew nuts

3 tablespoons low-sodium soy sauce

2 tablespoons rice vinegar

2 tablespoons chopped fresh ginger or 2 teaspoons ground ginger

1 teaspoon minced garlic

2 teaspoons cornstarch

Several drops hot sauce (optional)

4 teaspoons sesame oil, divided

Directions:

Place water for noodles on to boil. Cut mango into cubes. Place onion, red pepper, shrimp, snow peas, mango and cashew nuts on a cutting board in order of use. Mix soy sauce, rice wine vinegar, ginger, garlic, cornstarch and hot sauce (if desired) together in a small bowl.

When water comes to a boil, add noodles. Boil 2 minutes, drain and rinse under cold water. Set aside. Heat 2 teaspoons sesame oil in a wok or skillet over high heat. When oil is smoking, add the onion and red pepper.

Stir-fry 2 minutes. Add the shrimp and snow peas and stir-fry 1 minute.

Add the mango, cashews and sauce and stir-fry tossing all the ingredients together for 1 minute.

Remove to a plate. Add remaining 2 teaspoons oil and the noodles. Toss for 1 minute.

Divide noodles in half and place on dinner plates. Spoon shrimp, mango and vegetables over noodles.

Grilled Fish in Butter

Ingredients:

1 ½ Fish Fillets per person to be served

1 stick unsalted butter, melted

Bay Seasoning or seasoning salt and seasoning pepper

Directions:

Use a disposal baking pan or line an oblong cake pan with heavy foil.

Place fish in single layers in the pan.

Pour the melted butter over the fish and sprinkle with seasonings.

Get the grill very hot and put the pan on the grill. Once the butter is sizzling, turn fish over and over to cook through.

We use tilapia and keep cooking until the edges are crusty and brown. To me that is some of the best part of it.

Note: Wear an apron and stand back when flipping. Butter is very hot!

Bobbie's Taco Salad

Ingredients:

1 pound ground beef, sirloin or chuck

1 package of taco seasoning mix (I use original or mild)

1 can refried beans or black beans

1 can black olives, sliced

2 tomatoes, diced

1 onion diced

2 cups shredded cheese

Red French Salad Dressing

1 bag Doritos nacho chips, crushed

Directions:

Brown meat and cook with taco seasoning mix per instructions on package. Once that is done add the beans and olives, cheese, tomatoes and onion.

In big bowl, shred lettuce and add the combined ingredients. Toss together and add chips and dressing at the end.

Serve with guacamole and sour cream if desired.

You can also set out all ingredients separately and let everyone put together their own salad.

This is one of my Dad's favorites.

West Coast Turkey Burgers

Ingredients:

2 teaspoons olive oil

½ cup minced scallions

¾ teaspoon salt

¼ teaspoon black pepper

3 tablespoons sour cream

4 teaspoons Worcestershire sauce

1 ½ pounds lean ground turkey

3 ounce blue cheese (or Feta Cheese)

6 whole wheat hamburger buns

2 tomatoes, sliced

1 avocado, sliced

1 red onion, sliced

Directions:

Sauté scallions in a pan with the olive oil over medium heat until softened. Transfer to a medium bowl and season with the salt and pepper.

Stir in sour cream, Worcestershire sauce, and turkey and mix until just combined. Form into 6 patties

Heat a well oiled grill to medium high. Cook burgers until just cooked through, about 5 minutes on one side and 3 minutes on the other. Top each burger with some of the cheese and cook another 2 minutes or until burgers are fully cooked through and cheese is melted.

Top burgers with accouterments.

Broiled Salmon with Tomato Cream Sauce for two

This recipe is from Kim Bolt who says this is one of Tom's favorite dishes.

Ingredients:

2 - 6oz salmon fillets, salt and pepper

1 tablespoon butter

1/2 shallot finely chopped

1 tablespoons white wine or champagne vinegar

2 tablespoons tomato paste(**)

1/8 cup heavy cream

1/8 cup water

Directions:

Put salmon on a foil lined pan, season with salt and pepper.

Melt butter in a small saucepan, add shallots and cook until transparent 1-2 minutes.

Preheat broiler and then broil salmon until brown on top 6-8 minutes.

Add vinegar to the shallots and boil about 1 minute, then add tomato paste, heavy cream and water.

Simmer until thickened about 2 minutes or less- watch-it will easily burn. Drizzle sauce over salmon.

**using squeeze tube tomato paste is easy and not wasteful.

Crockpot Ham and Bean Soup

This is another of Kim Bolt's favorite recipes and I couldn't wait to make it. Wonderful!!!

Ingredients:

1 - large ham bone

2 cups dried beans NO NEED TO SOAK, measure dried beans in dry measure cup (a 16oz bag is too many beans. you can use any type, navy, great northern, I prefer 7 or 15 blend

4 cups chicken STOCK(not broth)**

1-2 cups water

1 bay leaf

3 small carrots

1 celery stalk

1 small onion

1 minced garlic clove or 1 tsp jarred minced garlic

salt and pepper to taste

1 package instant potatoes is optional.

Directions:

Put carrots, celery, onion and garlic in a food processor and grind up.

Add all to the Crockpot and cook 10-12 hours on low.

Discard bay leaf.

If you prefer thicker soup, and homemade bread crumbs or 1/2 package of instant potatoes to stock.

**She use Better Than Bouillon Chicken Base as you can make stock as you need it from the jar.

Carols Easy Crockpot Sauce for over Rice

This another recipe contributed by our friend, Kim Bolt.

Ingredients:

1 pound stew meat cut into SMALL cubes

1 package of Lipton dry onion soup mix

1 can Campbell cream of mushroom soup

1 cup red wine(any kind).

Directions:

Put all in the Crockpot, mix and cook on low 8hrs. serve over rice. Makes 4 large servings.

Barbecued Salmon with Fresh Nectarine Salsa

Ingredients:

4 4 to 5 ounce fresh frozen skinless salmon fillets, about 1 inch thick

3 tablespoons bottled barbecue sauce

1 ½ cups chopped nectarines (2 medium)

¾ cup fresh blueberries

¼ cup coarsely chopped pecans, toasted

Lemon wedges

Directions:

Thaw salmon, if frozen. Rinse salmon; pat dry with paper towels. Lightly sprinkle salmon with salt and ground black pepper. Place 2 tablespoons of the barbecue sauce in a small bowl; brush sauce onto both sides of the salmon.

For a charcoal or gas grill, place salmon on the greased rack of a covered grill directly over medium heat. Grill for 8 to 12 minutes or until salmon flakes when tested with a fork, turning once halfway through grilling.

For nectarine salsa, in a medium bowl combine nectarines, blueberries, pecans and the remaining 1 tablespoon barbecue sauce. Season to taste with salt. Serve salmon with salsa and lemon wedges.

Crock Pot Lasagna

Ingredients:

1 pound Ground Beef

Lasagna noodles

1 jar spaghetti sauce

1 1/2 cups cottage cheese

1 1/2 cups shredded Mozzarella cheese

2 tablespoons grated Parmesan cheese

Directions:

Brown ground beef and drain. Spoon 1 cup spaghetti sauce in bottom of 4 quart crock pot.

Mix remaining sauce with beef.

Place 2 uncooked lasagna noodles on sauce in crock pot.

Spread 1/3 meat mixture on top of noodles.

Spread 3/4 cup cottage cheese over meat.

Sprinkle 1/2 cup mozzarella cheese over cottage cheese.

Add another layer of uncooked noodles, 1/3 meat mixture, the remaining cottage cheese and 1/2 cup mozzarella cheese.

Place another layer of uncooked noodles, meat mixture, and mozzarella cheese.

Sprinkle Parmesan cheese over top. Cook on low for 4 hours.

If cooked much longer, it gets a bit well done.

Crock Pot Lasagna #2

Ingredients:

1 lb. lean ground beef

1 onion, chopped

2 garlic cloves, smashed

1 (28 oz.) can tomato sauce

1 (6 oz.) can tomato paste

1 1/2 tsp. salt 1 tsp. dried oregano

12 oz. cottage cheese

1/2 cup grated Parmesan cheese

12 oz. lasagna pasta, uncooked

16 oz. shredded mozzarella cheese

Directions:

Brown ground beef, onion and garlic in fry pan.

Add tomato sauce, tomato paste, salt and oregano.

Cook long enough to get it warm. Spoon a layer of meat sauce onto the bottom of the slow cooker.

Add a double layer of uncooked lasagna noodles (break to fit) and top with cheeses.

Repeat with sauce, noodles and cheeses until all are used up.

Cover and cook on low for 4 to 5 hours.

Ready in 4¼ hours.

Fish Tacos

Ingredients:

½ cup sour cream

½ cup mayonnaise

¼ cup chopped fresh cilantro

1 package taco seasoning mix, divided

1 pound cod or any white fish (I use tilapia) cut into 1 inch pieces

2 tablespoons vegetable oil

2 tablespoons lemon juice

1 (12 count) packages taco shells, warmed or 1 (12 count) packages flour tortillas

Toppings:

Shredded cabbage

Chopped tomato

Lime juice

Taco sauce

Directions:

Combine sour cream, mayonnaise, cilantro and 2 tablespoons seasoning mix in small bowl.

Combine fish, vegetable oil, lemon juice and remaining seasoning mix in medium bowl; pour into large skillet.

Cook, stirring constantly, over medium-high heat for 4 to 5 minutes or until fish flakes easily when tested with a fork.

Fill taco shells with fish mixture.

Top with toppings.

Easy, Tasty Pulled Pork

Directions:

Take a Hormel pork roast or any packaged pork roast and place it on 3 layers of aluminum foil.

Before closing up the foil, pour 1/3 cup of bar-b-que sauce over the roast.

Close up the foil and place in crock pot with a small amount of water to cause steam.

Cook on high for about 5 hours.

Unwrap foil over a large bowl, catching all the juices and meat in the foil.

Separate the meat with forks while mixing in the juices.

Serve hot on bun or just by itself.

I discovered this recipe by accident. It is so very flavorful and easy we probably won't go to any bar-b-que places again!!

Asian Pot Roast with Sweet and Sour Sauce

Pot Roast Ingredients:

2.5 pounds chuck cut into pieces

1 cup sugar

½ cup chopped garlic

2 bunches of chopped green onions

3 cups soy sauce

3 cups water

½ cup sesame oil

Directions:

Combine all ingredients in roasting dish or pan and cover with aluminum foil. Place in oven 350 degree oven for 3 hours. (I have done this in a crock pot and let it on high for several hours and it was very good.)

Sweet and Sour Sauce Ingredients:

1 cup pineapple juice

¾ cup water

½ pineapple medium diced (canned works)

1 mango medium diced

1 red pepper medium diced

1 green pepper medium diced

1 cup onion medium diced

¼ cup ketchup

2 ounce chopped garlic

1 ounce soy sauce

1/3 cup light brown sugar

4 tablespoons vegetable oil

4 tablespoons cornstarch

5 tablespoons of water

In a medium sauce pot, add oil, onion, garlic and peppers. Cook on medium heat until translucent.

Add remaining ingredients and bring to a boil stirring occasionally.

Reduce heat and simmer for approximately 10 minutes. Add cornstarch/water mixture slowly while stirring to desired thickness. You may not need it all.

(If I do the roast in the crock pot, I add the sweet and sour ingredients during the last hour of cooking and add the cornstarch the last 15 minutes to let it thicken.)

Makes 4 generous portions

Chinese Pork Chops

Ingredients:

½ cup soy sauce

¼ cup brown sugar

2 tablespoons lemon juice

1 tablespoon vegetable oil

½ teaspoon ground ginger

1/8 teaspoon garlic powder

6 boneless pork chops

Directions:

In bowl, mix soy sauce, brown sugar, lemon juice, vegetable oil, ginger, and garlic powder. Set aside some of the mixture in a separate bowl for marinating during cooking. Pierce the pork chops on both sides with a fork, place in a large plastic bag, and cover with the remaining marinade mixture. Refrigerate 6 to 8 hours.

Preheat the grill for high heat.

Lightly oil the grill grate. Discard marinade and grill pork chops 6 to 8 minutes per side or to desired doneness, marinating often with the reserved portion of marinade.

Maple-Brined Pork

Ingredients:

3 cups water

½ cup fat-free, low-sodium chicken broth

1 tablespoon black peppercorns

1 ½ teaspoons whole allspice

Garlic cloves, crushed

1 bay leaf, crushed

2 tablespoons plus ½ teaspoon kosher salt, divided

2 ½ tablespoons maple syrup, divided

Cooking spray

2 tablespoons butter, melted

2 ripe plums, halved and pitted

2 ripe peaches, halved and pitted

2 green onions, sliced (optional)

Directions:

Place first 6 ingredients, 2 tablespoons salt and 2 tablespoon syrup in a pan. Bring to a boil; dissolve salt. Cool. Seal pork and brine in a zip lock bag. Chill 8 hours; drain.

Preheat grill to medium-high heat.

Sprinkle pork with ¼ teaspoon ground pepper. Grill pork on a rack coated with cooking spray 3 minutes on each side or until done. Combine 1 ½ teaspoons syrup and butter; brush onto fruit, cut sides down, on rack coated with cooking spray for 3 minutes. Cut each peach and plum half in half again; serve with pork. Top with onions, if desired.

My daughter, April, says this is a great recipe. Came from Cooking Light magazine.

Chicken Pot Pie

Ingredients:

1 10 ounce can Campbell's cream of chicken soup or Campbell's chicken or turkey pot pie soup

1 ½ cups frozen mixed vegetables, thawed

1 ½ cups cubed, cooked chicken

¾ cup chicken broth combined with 3 tablespoons flour

2 Pillsbury pie shells

Directions:

Preheat oven to 400

Mix soup, vegetables, chicken and broth. The mixture should be somewhat thick. If only chicken noodle soup is available, it may be pureed in the blender to make a smooth gravy.

Put mixture into the bottom pie shell. Cover with the top pie crust and crimp to seal. Slice a few vent holes in the top.

Bake for 40 minutes or until golden brown. Cover pie edge with aluminum foil or a pie shield if it begins to brown too quickly.

My Daughter, April, gave me this recipe.

Bobbie's Meatballs (Meatloaf)

My meatball recipe is the same recipe for my meatloaf but since my loving husband refuses to eat meatloaf I make it into balls and he loves them.

Ingredients:

1 pound ground sirloin or ground chuck

1 envelope Lipton Onion soup (or any dry onion soup)

1 sleeve of soda crackers crushed

1 egg

1 cup ketchup (or amount to make consistency to hold together)

Directions:

Mix all of the ingredients together well and once it is all mixed up, form meat balls to desired size or form into a loaf and put into a loaf pan.

Bake in the oven until done to 170 degrees at 350 degrees.

Sometimes I place the meat balls when I make them small into the crock pot or pan on stove and cover them with a favorite bottled spaghetti sauce and simmer. Pasta can be served with the meatballs or they can just be eaten as is. Great for pot lucks.

Maxine's Pork Hangovers

Aunt Maxine made these all the time. Very easy and extremely tasty!

Ingredients:

4 thin boneless pork chops or pork loin, pounded thin

1 or 2 eggs, beaten

Cracker crumbs for coating; crushed fine (she used the round Ritz like crackers

Salt and Pepper

Cooking oil

Directions:

Preheat oil in skillet to medium high heat.

Pound pork thin, salt and pepper, dredge into egg mixture and then roll in cracker crumbs.

Place in hot oil and fry until nice and brown and turn and do the other side the same.

Drain on plate with a paper towel.

Serve as is or put in a whole wheat bun with lettuce, tomato, onion, pickles and mayo.

SIDE DISHES

Easy Broccoli & Cheddar Casserole

Ingredients:

2 cups white rice

15 oz. can Campbell's cream of mushroom soup

8 oz. shredded cheddar cheese

1 head broccoli florets (coarsely chopped)

1/2 cup chicken broth

1 tsp. Sea salt

1/2 tsp. black pepper

Directions:

Cook 2 cups of rice according to directions on box (after cooking should get 4 cups). Remove from heat and set aside. Add cream of mushroom soup and mix well.

In a pot of salted boiling water, blanch broccoli for about 3 minutes. Drain water well and keep warm.

Pre-heat oven to 350 degrees.

Add broccoli, chicken broth, cream of mushroom soup, Sea salt, black pepper, and cheddar cheese to rice & mix well. Pour into a well sprayed casserole & bake covered in oven for 40 minutes or until bubbly. Remove cover & bake additional 10 minutes until golden brown.

Garlic-Mint Peas

Ingredients:

1 pound sugar snap peas (2 cups)
2 cloves garlic, halved
1 tablespoon canola oil
2 cups fresh or thawed frozen peas
1/4 cup fresh mint leaves, chopped, or 1 tablespoon dried mint
1/2 teaspoon sugar
1/2 teaspoon salt

Directions:

Heat a large saucepan of water to boiling.

Add the snap peas and cook 2 to 3 minutes. Drain and rinse under running cold water.

In a large skillet over medium-low heat, cook the garlic in the oil until golden. Remove and discard the garlic.

Add the sugar snap peas and fresh or thawed peas and cook until tender, 3 to 5 minutes.

Remove from heat and add the mint, sugar, and salt.

Mexican Rice

This recipe is from Karen Sherman from Alligator Park in Punta Gorda, Florida

Ingredients:

2 cups water

2 cubes chicken bouillon

1 ½ cup brown rice

1 cup salsa

Directions:

Bring water, salsa and bouillon to boil. Add brown rice and cover. Simmer on low for 45 minutes.

Tomato Pie

Ingredients:

5-6 Tomatoes, peeled and sliced

Pie crust, baked per instructions

Salt and Pepper

Bake a frozen or fresh pie shell and set aside.

½ cup Mayo

2 cups shredded cheddar cheese, I use sharp

Fresh basil to taste, chopped

Directions:
Slice and peel Tomatoes. Put on nice layer on bottom of pie shell and salt and pepper.

Place another layer of Tomatoes and salt and pepper. Number of layers depends on the depth of the pie shell.

Mix Miracle whip with shredded cheese and fresh basil chopped.

Spread mixture over tomatoes and bake in a 350 degree oven for 40 minutes or until nicely browned.

Cut and serve. Will be a little juicy in the inside.

This can be eaten for breakfast, brunch, lunch or dinner or even a snack. We eat it as a meal but most people would probably like it as a side dish.

Creamed Spinach

Ingredients:

½ cup Hidden Valley® Original Ranch® Light Dressing

½ cup milk

½ teaspoon vegetable oil

black pepper to taste

1 teaspoon garlic powder to taste

2 packages (10 ounces) frozen spinach

4 teaspoons flour

Directions:

Cook spinach in microwave as package directs, then drain.

Meanwhile, mix the oil, flour, and milk in a sauce pan, stirring to remove any lumps. Heat over low to medium heat stirring constantly until mixture thickens, or about 10 minutes. Remove from heat.

Add Hidden Valley® The Original Ranch® Light Dressing, black pepper and garlic powder (if using), and cooked spinach.

Stir to combine.

Smashed Potatoes

Ingredients:

½ cup milk

1 packet (1 ounce) Hidden Valley® Original Ranch® Salad Dressing & Seasoning Mix

3 tablespoons butter or margarine

4 medium potatoes with or without skins

Directions:

Pierce skin of potatoes with fork; microwave 8 to 10 minutes or until tender.

Mash with fork. Add dressing mix, milk and butter to potatoes; stir well.

Veggie Fries

Ingredients:

½ cup olive oil plus 1 tablespoon

1 cup Hidden Valley® Original Ranch® Dressing plus extra for dipping

1 pound hard vegetables sliced into sticks, (carrots, red peppers, zucchini, green beans, and asparagus)

2 tablespoons fresh lemon juice

Directions:

Blanch vegetables in salted boiling water for 3 minutes to soften.

Mix dressing, olive oil and lemon juice.

Pour mixture over vegetables to coat.

Marinate for 1 to 3 hours.

Put 1 tablespoon of olive oil in a large frying pan.

Fry vegetables over medium heat until cooked through and brown on all sides.

Serve with dressing for dipping.

Angel Hair Pasta with Garlic, Herbs and Parmesan

Ingredients

8 ounces angel hair pasta

Salt

1/4 cup olive oil

2 Tbsp finely chopped fresh herbs such as rosemary, thyme, oregano

1/4 cup chopped fresh parsley

3 cloves of garlic, sliced

1/8 teaspoon chili pepper flakes (or more to taste)

1/2 to 1 teaspoon of freshly ground black pepper (to taste)

1/2 cup grated Parmesan cheese

Directions:

Bring a large pot of salted water to a boil. (1 Tbsp salt for every 2 quarts of water).

While the water is heating in step 1, heat the olive oil in a small saucepan on medium heat. Add the sliced garlic, chili pepper flakes, finely chopped herbs, and chopped parsley to the oil. Cook for one minute or until the parsley has wilted and the garlic is emitting a strong fragrance. Remove from heat.

The angel hair pasta will cook in about 2 minutes once it starts, so get everything ready. Once the water is at a rolling boil, add the pasta. Cook at a rolling boil until al dente. Drain the pasta and rinse briefly with cold water, just enough to stop the cooking, but not so much as to make the pasta cold. The pasta should still be quite warm.

Place pasta in a large bowl. Pour herbed garlic sauce over the pasta and gently toss to combine. Sprinkle Parmesan cheese and freshly ground black pepper over the pasta and gently toss to combine.

Serve immediately as a side dish. Reheats well if you make ahead.

Cheesy Cauliflower Au Gratin

This recipe is from Kay Atherton from Alligator Park in Punta Gorda, Florida.

Ingredients:

1 box frozen cauliflower flowerets

1 can cheese soup

1 cup 4 cheese, shredded

¼ teaspoon cayenne pepper

¼ teaspoon salt

Directions:

Place cauliflower in baking dish. Combine cheese soup, shredded cheese, pepper and salt. Pour over cauliflower and mix together. Microwave until heated through.

Baked Beans from Scratch

Ingredients:

1 pound dry cannellini, borlotti or Great Northern beans

1 Tbsp olive oil

1/4 pound bacon or pancetta, roughly chopped

1/2 medium onion, chopped

4 garlic cloves, chopped

1 Tbsp fresh sage, minced (can sub fresh rosemary)

1/2 to 1 teaspoon chile flakes (depending on how spicy you want it)

2 Tbsp honey

1/4 cup tomato paste

1 15-ounce can crushed tomatoes or tomato sauce

2 cups beef or chicken stock (use gluten-free stock for gluten-free version)

Salt

1/2 cup chopped fresh parsley

2 Tbsp balsamic vinegar

Directions:

Pre-soak the beans, either by covering with two inches of water and soaking overnight, or by pouring boiling water over them and soaking them for an hour.

Drain the beans and put them in a medium-sized pot and cover with 2 inches of water. Bring to a simmer, cover, reduce the heat to a low simmer and cook until the beans are just soft enough to eat, about 1 hour, give or take 15 minutes or so, depending on how old the beans are (older beans will take longer to cook).

Preheat the oven to 325°F. In a 3 or 4 quart heavy-bottomed, oven-proof, lidded pot such as a Dutch oven, heat the olive oil over medium heat. Add the bacon or pancetta and cook slowly until lightly browned and crispy.

Add the chopped onions and increase the heat to medium-high. Cook, stirring often, until the onions begin to brown. Use a wooden spoon to scrape any browned bits off the bottom of the pot.

Add the garlic, chile flakes and sage and cook for 1-2 minutes, then add the honey and tomato paste. Stir well to combine. Add the tomatoes or tomato sauce and the stock. Bring to a simmer. Taste for salt and add some if needed.

Drain the beans and add them to the pot. Stir well. Cover the pot and cook in the oven for an hour and fifteen minutes. If still a bit wet, remove the cover and cook for 15 minutes more. Note that the cooking time will depend on several things, the most important being how thoroughly the beans were cooked to begin with when they were simmered. If they are still a bit hard when they go in the oven, it may take several hours to soften them, once the tomato and honey have been added.

Right before serving, gently stir in the chopped parsley and balsamic vinegar. Taste for salt; add more if needed to taste.

Roasted Asparagus

Ingredients:

2 bunches asparagus (about 2 lbs.)

2 teaspoons olive oil

1/4 teaspoon salt

1/8 teaspoon freshly ground black pepper

1/3 cup packed freshly shredded parmesan cheese

2 teaspoons fresh lemon juice

Directions:

Preheat oven to 475°. Hold the end of an asparagus stalk and bend until it snaps off. Repeat with remaining stalks and discard woody ends.

Toss asparagus with olive oil, sprinkle with salt and pepper, and toss well.

Arrange asparagus in an even layer in a shallow baking dish. Sprinkle with parmesan cheese and bake until asparagus is crisp-tender and cheese is browned, about 10 minutes.

Sprinkle with lemon juice. Serve hot or warm.

Onion Pie

This recipe is from Lucille Moore from Crossett, Arkansas

Ingredients:

2 teaspoons butter or margarine

1 cup thinly sliced onions

1 unbaked 9 inch pie shell

3 eggs, slightly beaten

1 ½ teaspoons flour

2 teaspoons dry mustard

½ cup mayonnaise

1 cup cream or half and half, scalded

Directions:

Preheat oven to 350 degrees.

Sauté onions in butter until just tender. There is no reason you can't add something like spinach to the onions. Spread over unbaked pastry shell.

In medium bowl, combine remaining ingredients into warmed cream. Mix well and pour over onions. Bake about forty minutes.
Remove from oven and allow to stand 10 minutes before serving.

I personally add shredded cheese on top while it is standing.

Stovetop Mac n Cheese

Ingredients:

4 Tablespoons butter

¼ cup all-purpose flour

2 ½ cups whole milk

2 cloves garlic, peeled

12 ounces extra-sharp yellow Cheddar cheese, shredded

8 ounces pasteurized cheese product or yellow American cheese, cut into small cubes

1 pound elbow macaroni

Directions:

Heat medium saucepan of salted water to boiling on high.

In large saucepan, melt butter on medium. Sprinkle flour over melted butter. Cook 1 minute or until well combined, stirring constantly with wooden spoon. Reduce heat to medium low. While whisking, slowly drizzle milk into pan. Add garlic and ½ teaspoon salt. Heat sauce to simmering on medium or until thickened, whisking constantly.

By handfuls, add cheeses to sauce, stirring until melted before adding more. Remove from heat; discard garlic.

Cook pasta as label directs. Drain well, then stir into pan with cheese sauce and ¼ teaspoon alt. Serve immediately or transfer to a 3 quart baking dish. Cool, cover and refrigerate up to 3 days. Reheat, covered with foil, at 350 degrees until hot in center, about 1 hour.

Cheesy Cauliflower Patties

Ingredients:

1 head cauliflower

2 large eggs

1/2 c cheddar cheese, grated

1/2 c panko (found in the bread crumb aisle, healthier option)

1/2 t cayenne pepper (more of less to taste)

Salt

Olive oil

Directions:

Cut cauliflower into florets & cook in boiling water until tender about 10 minutes. Drain. Mash the cauliflower while still warm. Stir cheese, eggs, panko, cayenne & salt to taste.

Coat the bottom of a griddle or skillet with olive oil over medium-high heat.

Form the cauliflower mixture into patties about 3 inches across.

Cook until golden brown & set, about 3 minutes per side. Keep each batch warm in the oven while you cook the rest.

Mom's Scalloped Corn

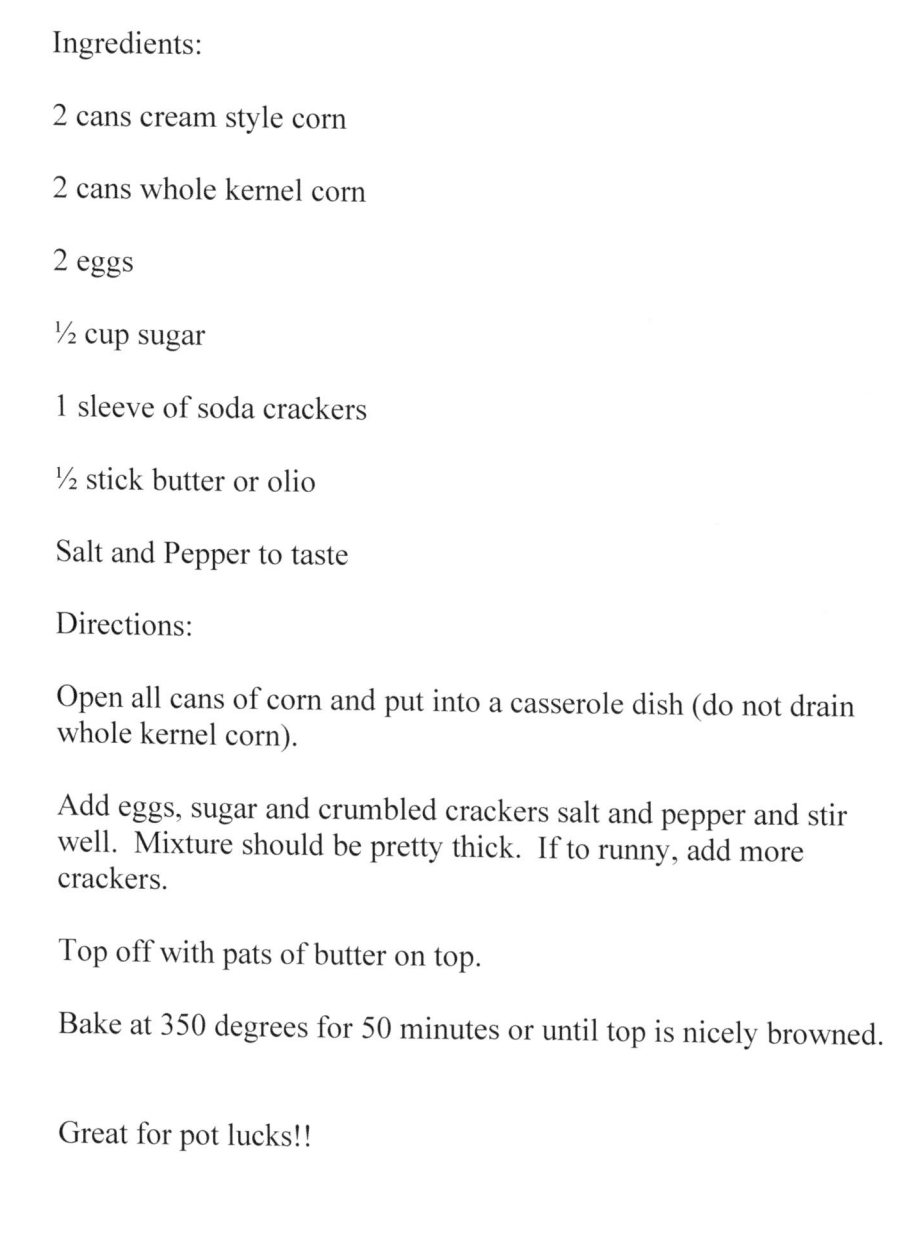

Ingredients:

2 cans cream style corn

2 cans whole kernel corn

2 eggs

½ cup sugar

1 sleeve of soda crackers

½ stick butter or olio

Salt and Pepper to taste

Directions:

Open all cans of corn and put into a casserole dish (do not drain whole kernel corn).

Add eggs, sugar and crumbled crackers salt and pepper and stir well. Mixture should be pretty thick. If to runny, add more crackers.

Top off with pats of butter on top.

Bake at 350 degrees for 50 minutes or until top is nicely browned.

Great for pot lucks!!

Vegetable Pie

Ingredients:

2 cups chopped broccoli or sliced fresh cauliflowerets
1/3 cup chopped onion
1/3 cup chopped green bell pepper
1 cup shredded Cheddar cheese (4 ounces)
1/2 cup Original Bisquick™ mix
1 cup milk
1/2 teaspoon salt
1/4 teaspoon pepper
2 eggs

Directions:

Heat oven to 400°F. Grease 9-inch pie plate. Heat 1 inch salted water to boiling in medium saucepan. Add broccoli; cover and heat to boiling. Cook about 5 minutes or until almost tender; drain thoroughly. Stir together cooked broccoli, onion, bell pepper and cheese in pie plate.

Stir remaining ingredients until blended. Pour into pie plate.

Bake 35 to 45 minutes or until golden brown and knife inserted in center comes out clean. Cool 5 minutes

DESSERTS

Marge's Cherry Cheesecake

Ingredients:

1 package of cream cheese, softened

½ box powdered sugar

1 frozen tub of whipped cream

1 large can of cherry pie filling

1 graham cracker crust

Directions:

Mix the cream cheese, powdered sugar and whipped cream together until smooth.

Pour into the pie crust

Pour cherry pie filling over the filling.

Refrigerate and cut when ready to eat.

Any fruit pie filling can be used instead of the cherry. Blueberry is great!

This is a dessert my mother, Marge Leininger, is expected to have whenever any of us kids visit!

Pink Lady

Ingredients:

1 large can fruit cocktail

1 8 oz. pkg. cream cheese

1 8 oz. Cool Whip

1/2 Cup chopped nuts (I used pecans)

One fourth cup cut-up maraschino cherries

Directions:

Fold together and enjoy.

From my dear friend, Norma Stanley

Two Ingredient Lemon Bars

Ingredients:

1 box angel food cake mix (I use Betty Crocker)

2 cans lemon pie filling

I used two 21 oz cans of Comstock pie filling (total of 42 ounces)

Directions:

Mix dry cake mix and cans of pie filling together in large bowl.
I just mixed it by hand...
Pour into greased 9 x 13" baking pan.
Bake at 350 degrees for 25 minutes or until top is starting to brown.

NOTE...Mine took the full 25 minutes to get done and did not brown on top at all.

Cool on wire rack and sprinkle with powdered sugar. It has a melt in your mouth spongy texture.

Reese's Peanut Butter No Bake Bars

Ingredients:

1 cup salted butter (melted)

2 cups graham cracker crumbs...

1/4 cup brown sugar

1 3/4 cup powdered sugar

1 cup peanut butter

1/2 tsp. vanilla

1 (11 oz) bag milk chocolate chips

Directions:

Combine all ingredients, except chocolate chips in a medium sized bowl. Stir until the mixture is smooth and creamy.

Pour peanut butter mixture into a 9 x 13 pan.

Melt chocolate chips in the microwave (at 50% power) for 1-2 minutes. Stir chocolate and pour over the peanut butter mixture. Spread chocolate with a spatula. To even out chocolate, tap pan on the counter.

Refrigerate bars for one hour. Cut while bars are still cool.

This recipe was posted on Facebook by my granddaughter Macie and they are really yummy.

Brownie Bowl Sundaes

Found this on my Facebook from Frank Snipes one day and it really looked like a great idea for a party or just to fancy up a simple dessert of ice cream sundaes!

Ingredients:

- Your favorite ice cream

- Your favorite brownie recipe

- Your favorite toppings

Directions:

Spray cups of a muffin tin with cooking spray, and add brownie batter to each cup until they're about two-thirds full.

Spray the second muffin tin with cooking spray and place on top of the first tin of brownies.

Bake!

Fill the brownie cups with ice cream and toppings. Instant party!

Ultimate Blueberry Cake/Coffee Cake

Ingredients:

2 cups Original Bisquik Mix

2 teaspoons baking powder

2 tablespoons vegetable oil

1 teaspoon vanilla

3 tablespoons sugar

1 cup milk

2 eggs

2 cups (or more if desired) blueberries fresh or frozen

Powdered sugar to dust top

Directions:

Mix all ingredients together except powdered sugar and fruit and pour into a greased 9 x 13 cake pan.

Drop fruit on top of batter.

Bake at 350 degrees or until golden brown on top and toothpick comes out clean.

If using a glass pan, bake at 325 degrees.

Dust with powder sugar and serve as cake or coffee cake.

Note: No reason why other fruit can't be used but we prefer the blueberries.

Pineapple Upside Down Cake in the Slow Cooker

Ingredients:

1/2 cup melted butter, divided

2/3 cup brown sugar

20 oz pineapple (crushed or tidbit), drained and juice reserved

1 white or yellow cake mix

Instructions:

Stir together 1/4 cup of butter (half of the amount listed), brown sugar and drained pineapple.

Spread this on bottom of slow cooker.

Stir the dry cake mix, remaining 1/4 melted butter and pineapple juice in a large bowl.

Pour cake batter over top of pineapple in slow cooker.

Bake on high for 2-3 hours or low for 3-4 hours.

Easy Apple Fritters

Ingredients:

1 cup all purpose flour

1/4 cup sugar

3/4 teaspoon salt

1 1/2 teaspoons baking powder

1 teaspoon cinnamon

1/3 cup milk

1 egg

1 cup chopped apple

Glaze:

2 cups powdered sugar

1 1/2 tablespoons milk

Directions:

Combine flour, sugar, salt, baking powder, cinnamon. Stir in milk and egg until just combined. Fold in apple. Pour oil into skillet so that it is approximately 1 1/2 deep. Heat oil on high. Oil is ready when a little dough thrown in floats to top.

Carefully add dough to oil in heaping teaspoons. Cook until brown, about 2 minutes, then flip. Cook another 1-2 minutes, until both sides are browned.

Transfer briefly to paper towels to absorb excess oil, then transfer to cooling rack.

Make glaze by stirring milk and powdered sugar together in a small bowl. Drizzle over apple fritters. Wait approximately 3 minutes for glaze to harden, then flip fritters and drizzle glaze over the other side. Best served warm.

Easy Pineapple Upside Down Cake

Cake Ingredients:

2 eggs

2/3 Cup white sugar

4 Tablespoon pineapple juice

2/3 Cup all purpose flour

1 teaspoon baking powder

1/4 teaspoon salt

Topping:

1/4 Cup butter (1/2 stick or 4 Tablespoons)

2/3 Cup brown sugar

1-can pineapple rings, crushed pineapple or pineapple pieces

6-maraschino cherries

Directions:

Preheat oven to 350 degrees. BAKE TIME 30 to 35 minutes

In a mixing bowl, add eggs, white sugar, and pineapple juice. Beat for 2 minutes. In a separate bowl, sift together the flour, baking powder, and salt. Add to the wet ingredients and turn mixer back on for 2 minutes.

In a small sauce pan, melt the butter and add the brown sugar. Stir on low heat for one minute. If you have a Teflon coated pan (about 8 inches) that is oven safe you can use this pan for finished product, otherwise pour mixture into greased baking pan.

Place pineapple on top of brown sugar mixture. Add cherries in with the pineapple. Pour cake mixture over and bake until a toothpick comes out of cake part clean.

Serve warm as is or top with vanilla ice cream or whipped cream.

Mexican Flan

Ingredients:

1 cup white sugar

3 eggs

1 (14 ounce) can sweetened condensed milk

1 (12 ounce) can evaporated milk

1 tablespoon vanilla extract

Directions:

Preheat oven to 350 degrees

In a medium saucepan over medium-low heat, melt sugar until liquefied and golden in color. Carefully pour hot syrup into a 9 inch round glass baking dish, turning the dish to evenly coat the bottom and sides. Set aside.

In a large bowl, beat eggs. Beat in condensed milk, evaporated milk and vanilla until smooth. Pour egg mixture into baking dish. Cover with aluminum foil.

Bake in preheated oven 60 minutes. Let cool completely.

To serve, carefully invert on serving plate with edges when completely cool.

Soft Oatmeal Cookies

Ingredients:

1 cup butter, softened

1 cup white sugar

1 cup packed brown sugar

2 eggs

1 teaspoon vanilla extract

2 cups all-purpose flour

1 teaspoon baking soda

1 teaspoon salt

1 1/2 teaspoons ground cinnamon

3 cups quick cooking oats

raisins or nuts (optional)

Directions:

In a medium bowl, cream together white sugar, butter, and brown sugar. Beat in eggs one at a time, and then stir in vanilla.

Combine flour, cinnamon, baking soda and salt. Stir into the creamed mixture. Mix in oats. If you are using nuts or raisins, mix into dough, combining well. Cover, and chill dough for at least one hour.

Preheat the oven to 375 degrees F (190 degrees C). Grease cookie sheets. Roll the dough into balls, and place 2 inches apart on cookie sheets.

Bake for 8 to 10 minutes in preheated oven. Allow cookies to cool on baking sheet for 5 minutes before transferring to a wire rack to cool completely.

Maxine's Grape Pie

Ingredients:

9 inch pie crust top and bottom

1/2 cup of sugar

1/3 cup of flour

1/2 teaspoon of cinnamon

4 cups of concord grapes cut in half

1 tablespoon of lemon juice

3 tablespoons of butter

Directions:

Stir sugar, flour and cinnamon together then mix with grapes.

Place in the pie crust and then sprinkle with lemon juice and dot with butter.

Cover with the top crust and cut slits in the crust and
Bake at 425 for 35 to 45 minutes or until a little bubbly.

Maxine's Peach Cobbler

Ingredients:

¾ cup margarine

2 cups white sugar

2 cups self rising flour

1 ¾ cups milk

¾ cup sugar

1 large can of peaches (any canned fruit will work for variation)

Directions:

Preheat oven to 350 degrees

Put margarine in 9 x 13 baking pan (oblong) and melt in oven while mixing together sugar, flour and milk. Pour over melted margarine – do not stir.

Pour undrained fruit over batter.

Sprinkle rest of sugar over the top.

Bake 30 to 40 minutes.

This was Great Grandma Leininger's recipe – Orpha Leininger

Maxine's Sugar Cookies

Ingredients:

3 cups sugar

1 ½ cups butter

5 eggs

1 ½ teaspoons vanilla

2 capfuls almond extract

6 ½ cups flour

3 tablespoons baking powder

½ teaspoon baking soda

½ teaspoon salt

1/12 cup sour cream

Directions:

Cream sugar and butter. Add eggs almond extract and vanilla. Alternate dry ingredients and sour cream.

Drop large tablespoons on a greased cookie sheet. Put sugar on top and press down slightly.

Bake at 350 for 10 to 12 minutes.

One Bowl Apple Cake

Ingredients:

2 eggs

1 3/4 cups sugar

2 heaping teaspoons cinnamon

1/2 cup oil

6 medium Gala or Fuji or Honey Crisp apples

2 cups flour

2 teaspoons baking soda

Directions:

Preheat oven to 350°. In a large bowl, mix the eggs, sugar, cinnamon and oil. Peel and slice the apples and add to mixture in bowl (coating as you go to keep apples from turning brown.)

Mix together the baking soda and flour and add to the ingredients in the bowl. Mix well (best with a fork) until all of the flour is absorbed by the wet ingredients.

Pour mixture into a greased one 9x13 or two 9" round pans. Bake for approximately 55 minutes.

Pepsi Cake

Ingredients:

2 cups flour

2 cups sugar

1 tsp. salt

2 tbsp. cocoa

1 tsp. baking soda

1 cup butter

1 cup Pepsi Cola

1/2 cup buttermilk

1 1/2 cups miniature marshmallows

2 eggs, beaten

Directions:

Combine flour, sugar, salt, cocoa and baking soda. In small saucepan, bring butter and Pepsi Cola to a boil. Add dry ingredients to mixture and then add buttermilk, eggs, and marshmallows to reach a thin batter. Bake in 9x12 inch baking pan at 350 degrees for about 45 to 60 minutes or until a toothpick comes out clean.

Topping for Pepsi cake:

1/2 cup (1 stick) butter

6 tbsp. Pepsi Cola

1 cup chopped nuts

1 tbsp. cocoa

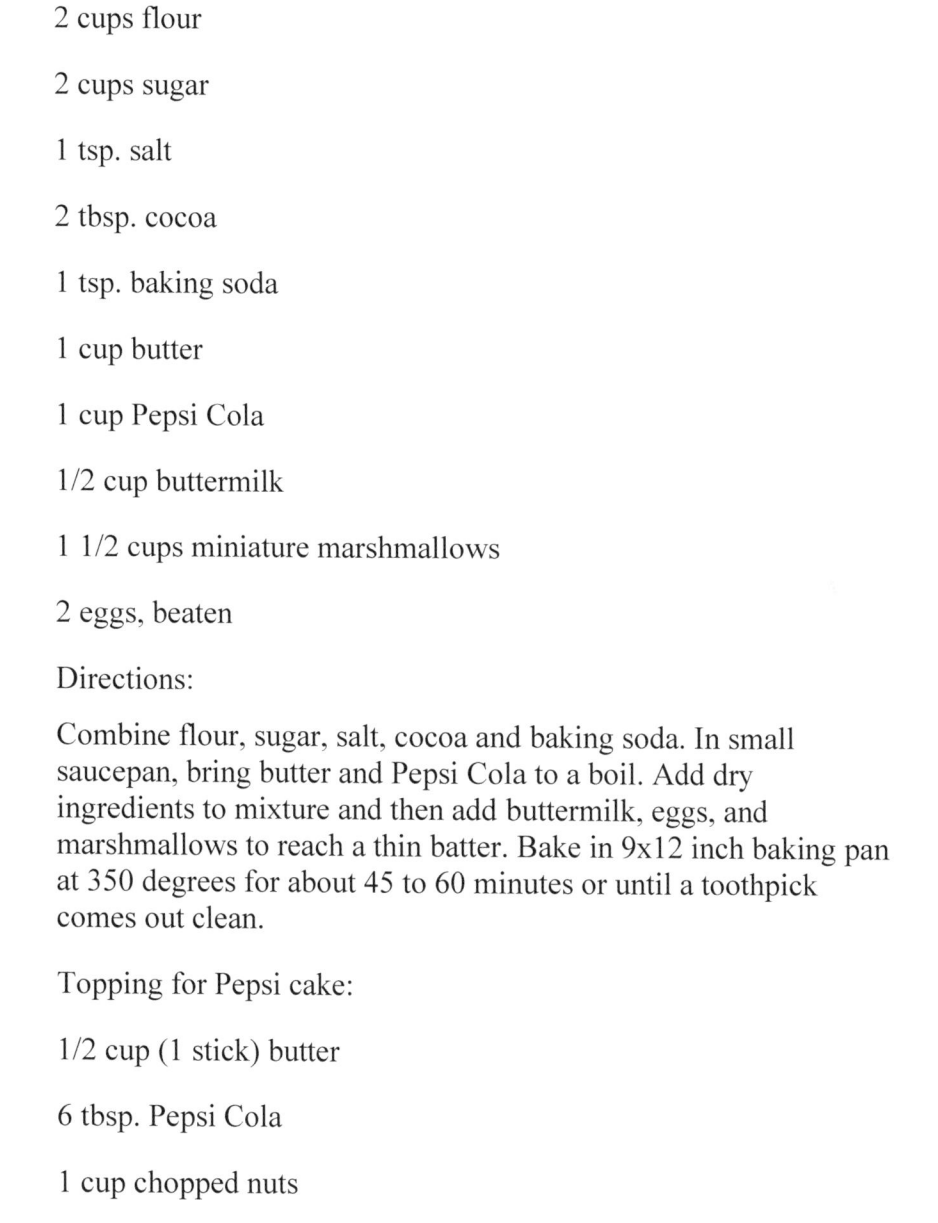

1 box confectioner's sugar

1 tsp. vanilla

Combine butter, cocoa and Pepsi in a small saucepan and bring to a boil. Pour over sugar and mix well. Add nuts and vanilla and pour over cake while still hot.

Chocolate Éclair Cake

Ingredients:

1 cup water

1/2 cup butter

1 cup flour

4 large eggs

1 (8 ounce) package cream cheese, softened

1 large box (5.1 ounces) vanilla instant pudding

3 cups milk

1 8 oz. container cool whip (you won't use the whole container) or one batch of homemade whipped cream

Chocolate syrup or homemade chocolate sauce

Directions:

Preheat oven to 400. Lightly grease a 9"X13" glass baking pan.

Éclair Crust: In a medium saucepan, melt butter in water and bring to a boil. Remove from heat. Stir in flour. Mix in one egg at a time, mixing completely before adding another egg. Spread mixture into pan, covering the bottom and sides evenly. *If the sides of your pan are too greased you won't be able to get the mixture to stay up the sides so make sure to just lightly grease.

Bake for 30-40 minutes or until golden brown (Mine only took 25 minutes.) You may want to check it occasionally-you don't want to overcook the crust, it will ruin the cake! Remove from oven and let cool (don't touch or push bubbles down).

Filling: Whip cream cheese in a medium bowl. In separate bowl make vanilla pudding. Make sure pudding is thick before mixing in with cream cheese. Slowly add pudding to cream cheese, mixing until there are no lumps.

Let cool in fridge. When the crust is completely cooled, pour filling in. Top with layer of cool whip however thick you want it and serve with chocolate syrup.

*If you want to make this even better use homemade whipped cream.

Apple Crisp

Ingredients:

4 medium tart cooking apples, sliced (4 cups)

3/4 cup packed brown sugar

1/2 cup Gold Medal™ all-purpose flour

1/2 cup quick-cooking or old-fashioned oats

1/3 cup butter or margarine, softened

3/4 teaspoon ground cinnamon

3/4 teaspoon ground nutmeg

Cream or Ice cream, if desired

Directions:

Heat oven to 375°F. Grease bottom and sides of 8-inch square pan with shortening.

Spread apples in pan. In medium bowl, stir remaining ingredients except cream until well mixed; sprinkle over apples.

Bake about 30 minutes or until topping is golden brown and apples are tender when pierced with a fork. Serve warm with cream.

To ensure recipe success if using a vegetable oil spread, use a spread with at least 65% vegetable oil.

Rise to the occasion! Self-rising flour can be used in this recipe.

If blueberry crisp is your cup of tea, simply use 4 cups fresh or frozen (thawed and drained) blueberries for the apples.

Funnel Cakes

Ingredients:

3 large eggs

1/4 cup sugar

2 cups milk

3 2/3 cups flour

1/2 teaspoon Salt

2 teaspoon baking powder

Vegetable oil

Directions:

Beat eggs and sugar together and then add the milk slowly--beat. Add the dry ingredients and beat until smooth and creamy.

Pour batter into a funnel and at the same time, use your finger to plug the hole. In a large cast iron pot, add 2 inches of oil to the bottom.

When the oil becomes hot, move your hand over the pot and slowly release your finger so the batter can start cooking.

Move the funnel around to make designs.

Brown on both sides--then immediately remove and drain extremely well.

This recipe was put on Facebook by my son-in-law, Kent Kilner.

BEVERAGES

Carrot Cake Cocktail

Ingredients:

1/3 Hot Shots (cinnamon schnapps)

1/3 Butter Shots (butterscotch schnapps)

1/3 Baileys (Irish cream)

Directions:

Serve over ice.

This drink recipe was given to me by the bartender at the Port St. Lucie's Eks lodge and it really does taste like a carrot cake!

Orange Julius

Ingredients:

6 ounces frozen orange juice concentrate

1 cup milk, low fat okay

1 cup water

1/4 cup sugar

1 teaspoon vanilla

8 ice cubes

Directions:

Combine all ingredients, except ice cubes, in blender.

Blend 1-2 minutes, adding ice cubes one at a time, until smooth.

Internal Detox for Glowing Skin

This is a great, simple drink to detox impurities from your body. It cleanses your body from the inside out. Extremely easy to drink too. Have one first thing in the morning, and one before bed. You will see the difference within a week. Try keeping this up for 1 week every month. If you can drink this every day, it would be WONDERFUL."

Ingredients:

2 1/2 teaspoons good quality honey

1 slice lemon, 1 inch

1 cup very hot water

Directions:

Add honey to the boiling mug of water, stir till completely dissolved.

Add the slice of lemon and allow it to brew for 5 minutes, stirring occasionally.

Sit back and enjoy the drink.

Southern Sweet Ice Tea

Ingredients:

6 regular tea bags

1/8 teaspoon baking soda

2 cups boiling water

1 1/2-2 cups sugar

6 cups cold water

Directions:

In a large glass measuring cup, place the tea bags and add the baking soda.

Pour the boiling water over the tea bags.

Cover and steep for 15 minutes.

Take out the tea bags and do not squeeze them.

Pour the tea mixture into a 2-quart pitcher; add the sugar.

Stir until the sugar is dissolved.

Add in the cold water.

Let cool; chill in the refrigerator and serve over ice.

Best Ever Lemonade

Ingredients:

1 ¾ cups white sugar

8 cups water

1 ½ cups lemon juice

Directions:

In a small saucepan, combine sugar and 1 cup water. Bring to boil and stir to dissolve sugar. Allow to cool to room temperature, then cover and refrigerate until chilled.

Remove seeds from lemon juice, but leave pulp. In pitcher, stir together chilled syrup, lemon juice and remaining 7 cups water.

Punch

Ingredients:

1 (64 ounce) can pineapple juice

1 (2 liter) 7-UP

1 package lemon-lime Kool-Aid

1 (2 pint) lime sherbet

Directions:

Make Kool-Aid according to package directions. Freeze in ring mold or ice cube trays.

In punch bowl, mix pineapple juice and 7-UP. Add frozen Kool-Aid and scoops of sherbet.

Beer Margarita

Ingredients:

1 – 12 ounce can frozen limeade concentrate

12 ounces tequila

12 ounces water

12 ounces beer

Ice

1 lime, cut into wedges

Directions:

Pour limeade, tequila, water and beer into a large pitcher. Stir until well blended, and limeade has melted.

Add plenty of ice and garnish with lime wedges. Adjust with additional water if needed.

Eggnog

Ingredients:

4 cups milk

5 whole cloves

½ teaspoon vanilla extract

1 teaspoon ground cinnamon

12 egg yolks

1 ½ cups sugar

2 ½ cups light rum

4 cups light cream

2 teaspoons vanilla extract

½ teaspoon ground nutmeg

Directions:

Combine milk, cloves, 1/2 teaspoon vanilla, and cinnamon in a saucepan, and heat over lowest setting for 5 minutes. Slowly bring milk mixture to a boil.

In a large bowl, combine egg yolks and sugar. Whisk together until fluffy. Whisk hot milk mixture slowly into the eggs. Pour mixture into saucepan. Cook over medium heat, stirring constantly for 3 minutes, or until thick. Do not allow mixture to boil. Strain to remove cloves, and let cool for about an hour.

Stir in rum, cream, 2 teaspoon vanilla, and nutmeg. Refrigerate overnight before serving.

English Channel

This yummy cocktail is from Tim Culey from Jonesboro, Arkansas

Ingredients:

¾ ounce Scotch

¾ ounce Irish Cream Liqueur

½ ounce Cointreau

Directions:

All ingredients should be chilled. Pour gently back and forth between two chilled containers. Pour into chilled glass over 1 ice cube. Garnish with strip of orange peel, if desired.

Old-School Melon Cocktails

Ingredients:

2/3 cup diced cantaloupe

¼ cup apple cider

1 lemon

Kosher salt

1 teaspoon honey

6 ounces neutral gin, chilled

Lemon wedges and melon balls, for garnish

Directions:

Puree the cantaloupe with the cider, the juice of ½ lemon and a pinch of salt in a blender at low speed. While you want the mixture to be smooth, keeping the blender on low will help avoid whipping unnecessary air into the melon and lightening the flavor along with the color. Add a little ice water if the blender has trouble blending the melon, and if you feel the melon lacks sweetness, add honey to taste.

Put half each of the melon puree and gin and 1 more tablespoon lemon juice in shaker with a few ice cubes and shake until blended and cold. Strain into 2 chilled glasses. Rub the rim of each glass with the lemon wedge for a little added acidity when sipping and garnish with melon balls.

Makes 2 drinks

Peanut Butter-Nana-Strawberry Smoothie

This is a recipe from Kim Souza from Ventura, California

Ingredients:

2 tablespoons creamy peanut butter

1 banana, peeled

5 fresh medium strawberries, hulled

½ cup plain non-fat yogurt

10 ice cubes

Directions:

Place peanut butter, banana, strawberries, yogurt and ice cubes in blender. Puree until smooth.

Electric Lemonade

Ingredients:

1 cup freshly squeezed lemon juice

1 cup sparkling mineral water

½ cup fresh mint leaves

¼ to ½ cup sugar

Dash ginger ale

2 to 3 cups ice

1 cup vodka

Lemon slices (optional)

Directions:

Chill four tall glasses in the freezer. In a blender combine lemon juice, sparkling water, mint, sugar to taste and ginger ale. Add ice. Cover and slowly blend until thick.

Remove glasses from freezer; if desired, add lemon slices. Pour ¼ cup of vodka into each glass. Top with frozen lemonade mixture.

CONDIMENTS

Fresh Salsa

Ingredients:

½ cups chopped white onion

3 diced tomatoes

1 diced seeded jalapeno

1 minced garlic clove

1/3 cup chopped cilantro

Directions:

Soak onion in cold water for 15 minutes and drain.

Toss onion with all other ingredients.

Add lime juice and salt to taste.

Spicy Garlic Dressing

This recipe came from Marjorie Ross from Paragon, Indiana

Ingredients:

1 cup sugar

¼ cup apple cider

1 tablespoon cold water

½ teaspoon onion salt

1 teaspoon garlic salt

½ teaspoon celery salt

1 teaspoon seasoned salt

¼ teaspoon black pepper

¼ teaspoon celery seed

½ cup vegetable oil (approximately)

Directions:

Mix all ingredients except oil and set aside for several hours to let the flavors combine. Then measure mixture in measuring cup and add ½ as much oil as you have sugar/vinegar mixture. Refrigerate for several hours before serving.

Grilled Pineapple Salsa

Ingredients:

1 sliced pineapple, grilled and then chopped

½ cup chopped white onion

2 diced tomatoes

1 diced seeded jalapeno

1 minced garlic clove

1/3 cup chopped cilantro

1 teaspoon grated ginger

Directions:

Soak onion in cold water for 15 minutes and drain.

Grill pineapple on a grill until charred and chop. Toss onion and pineapple with all other ingredients.

Add lime juice and salt to taste.

Creamy Cucumber Salsa

Ingredients:

2 cups diced seeded, cucumber

¼ cup chopped cilantro

¼ cup chopped scallions

1 diced seeded Serrano chile

½ teaspoon ancho chile powder

½ teaspoon cumin

¼ cup crema

Lime juice and salt to taste

Directions:

Toss all together

Lobster Salsa

Ingredients:

1 ½ cups diced cooked lobster meat

2 cups diced seeded, cucumber

¼ cup chopped cilantro

¼ cup chopped scallions

1 diced seeded Serrano chile

½ teaspoon ancho chile powder

½ teaspoon cumin

¼ cup crema

Lime juice and salt to taste

Directions:

Toss all together

Black Bean Salsa

Ingredients:

1 can black beans, drained and rinsed

1 cup diced tomatoes

2 diced seeded jalapenos

¼ cup chopped cilantro

¼ cup chopped scallions

1 minced garlic clove

1 chopped chipotle in adobo sauce plus 2 tablespoon of sauce

Lime juice

Salt

Directions:

Mix all ingredients and add lime juice and salt to taste.

Fruit Salsa

Ingredients:

¾ cup diced strawberries

¾ cup diced cantaloupe

¾ cup diced grapes

Juice of ½ lime

Juice of ½ orange

1 teaspoon honey

2 tablespoons chopped mint

2 tablespoons chopped basil

Directions:

Mix all ingredients together.

Coney Dog Sauce

Ingredients:

2 pounds hamburger

3 Tablespoons mustard

2 Tablespoon salt

3 Tablespoons Chili Powder

3 Tablespoons Garlic Powder

1 Teaspoon crushed Pepper

1 large can tomato paste

1 large can tomato puree

2 Cups water

Directions:

Blend all ingredients. Simmer for 3 hours or start in crock pot and put on high for 5 hours.

Strawberry Freezer Jam

Ingredients:

1 quart (4 cups) strawberries, cut in half
4 cups sugar
3/4 cup water
1 package (1 3/4 ounces) powdered fruit pectin

Directions:

Mash strawberries with potato masher or in food processor until slightly chunky (not pureed) to make 2 cups crushed strawberries. Mix strawberries and sugar in large bowl. Let stand at room temperature 10 minutes, stirring occasionally.

Mix water and pectin in 1-quart saucepan. Heat to boiling, stirring constantly. Boil and stir 1 minute. Pour hot pectin mixture over strawberry mixture; stir constantly 3 minutes.

Immediately spoon mixture into freezer containers, leaving 1/2-inch headspace. Wipe rims of containers; seal. Let stand at room temperature about 24 hours or until set.

Store in freezer up to 6 months or in refrigerator up to 3 weeks. Thaw frozen jam and stir before serving.

Ketchup Variations

These are just a few different ways to spice up your everyday ketchup to compliment any food!

Five-Spice Ketchup Mix 1 cup ketchup, the juice of 1 lime and 2 teaspoons five-spice powder. Season with salt and pepper.

Curry Ketchup Cook 1/4 cup minced onion in a saucepan with 1 tablespoon butter until soft, 3 minutes. Add 1 teaspoon each curry powder and paprika and a pinch of cayenne; cook until toasted, 1 minute. Add 1 cup ketchup and 1/2 cup water; simmer until thick, about 25 minutes.

Spicy Peanut Ketchup Mix 3/4 cup ketchup, 1/3 cup peanut butter, the juice of 1 lime, 1 tablespoon harissa or other chile paste and 1/4 teaspoon each coriander, smoked paprika, cinnamon and cayenne.

Bloody Mary Ketchup Mix 3/4 cup ketchup, 1/4 cup horseradish, 2 teaspoons hot sauce, 1 teaspoon celery salt and 1/2 teaspoon Worcestershire sauce.

Sun-Dried Tomato Ketchup Puree 1/2 cup sun-dried tomatoes with 1 tablespoon of the oil from the jar, 2 tablespoons cider vinegar, 1 tablespoon brown sugar, 1/4 teaspoon each cayenne and ground ginger and 1/4 cup water until smooth.

Scallion-Bacon Ketchup Cook 4 slices diced bacon until crisp; drain on paper towels, reserving the drippings. Mix 3/4 cup ketchup, 1/4 cup chopped scallions, the bacon and 1 tablespoon each bacon drippings and Worcestershire sauce.

Roasted Garlic Mustard Wrap 8 cloves garlic in foil; roast 30 minutes at 400 degrees F. Squeeze the garlic out of its skin and puree with 1/2 cup Dijon mustard, 1/3 cup maple syrup, and salt and pepper.

Jerk Ketchup Mix 3/4 cup ketchup, 2 tablespoons jerk seasoning, 1 tablespoon pineapple or peach preserves and 1 tablespoon lime juice.

Dill Mustard Mix 1/2 cup yellow mustard, 1/4 cup each finely chopped dill pickles and white onions, and 1 tablespoon chopped fresh dill.

Stout Mustard Mix 2 tablespoons stout beer, 1/4 cup each whole-grain and Dijon mustard, 1/2 minced small shallot and 2 teaspoons brown sugar.

Honey Soy Marinade

Ingredients:

1 tablespoon packed brown sugar

1 tablespoon butter or margarine, melted

1 tablespoon olive or vegetable oil

1 tablespoon honey

1 tablespoon soy sauce

1 clove garlic, finely chopped

Directions:

In small bowl, mix all ingredient.

This marinade is great on salmon but works well on pork as well.

In shallow glass or plastic dish, place meat. Pour marinade over meat. Cover and refrigerate at least 30 minutes but no longer than 1 hour.

Bake, roast or grill as desired.

MISCELLANEOUS

Miracle Granola

Ingredients:

6 cups Quick Cooking Oatmeal

¼ cup sesame seed (optional)

½ cup honey

¾ cup brown sugar

½ cup chopped walnuts

½ cup slivered almonds

¾ cup wheat germ

½ cup salad oil

½ teaspoon salt

¾ cup coconut

1 ½ teaspoon vanilla

Directions:

Preheat oven to 325 degrees. Put oatmeal in large ungreased cookie pan. Bake oatmeal 12 minutes. In large bowl, put baked oatmeal and other ingredients in and mix well. Divide in half. Put in large pans and bake in oven for ½ hour. Stir frequently. Add raisins, dates or other dried fruits. Cool thoroughly. Put in glass or plastic containers with tight fitting lids. Store in refrigerator.

This can be eaten as a cold cereal with milk. It is a good snack food, full of nutrition. Can be sprinkled over cooked cereal; or used as a topping for ice cream or pudding or a tasty topping for coffee cakes and yogurt.

Bread and Butter Slices

Ingredients:

4 cups medium-size sliced cucumbers (do not peel)

6 medium white onions, sliced

2 green peppers, sliced

3 cloves of garlic

Directions:

Cover these with crushed ice for 3 hours.

Then mix:

½ cup salt

5 cups sugar

1 ½ teaspoons turmeric

1 ½ teaspoons celery seed

2 tablespoons yellow mustard seed

3 cups cider vinegar

Mix thoroughly and pour over cucumber mixture. Heat to a boil, but do not boil. Seal in hot sterilized pint jars.

Makes 8 pints.

Flea Fighter Fingers Dog Cookies

This dough is very easy to handle. It makes a nice, dark biscuit and helps your pet repel fleas because of the presence of brewer's yeast. Makes about 100 small cookies.

Ingredients:

2 beef bouillon cubes

1 ¾ cups boiling water

1 ½ cups all purpose flour

1 ½ cups whole wheat flour

1 cup rye flour

1 cup quick cooking rolled oats

1 cup cornmeal, stone ground

¼ cup brewer's yeast

2 Tablespoons garlic powder

½ cup vegetable oil

1 egg, beaten

Directions:

In a 2 cup measuring cup, dissolve bouillon cubes in boiling water and set aside until room temperature.

In a large mixing bowl, combine dry ingredients.

Make a well in the flour mixture and gradually stir in oil, egg and bouillon until well blended.

Divide dough into 2 balls, so it is easy to work with.

Knead each dough ball on a floured surface, about 3-4 minutes.

With a rolling pin, roll dough to between ¼ inch and ½ inch thickness.

Cut with small cutter and place on a baking sheet, lined with foil. Bake 1 ½ hours at 300 degrees.

Cool on a rack until hard and store, at room temperature, in a container with a loose-fitting lid.

Economy Dog Cookies

Easy and economical to make. A nice, light, beige cookie. Makes about 50 using a small cutter.

Ingredients:

1/3 cup margarine or butter
3 cups whole wheat flour
½ cup powdered skim milk
¼ tsp garlic powder
¾ cup water, room temperature
1 egg beaten

Directions:

In a large mixing bowl, cream margarine and flour with a pastry cutter and set aside.

In a small bowl, dissolve powdered skim milk and garlic powder in water and whisk in beaten egg.

Make a well in the flour mixture and gradually stir in egg mixture until well blended.

Knead dough on a floured surface, about 3-4 minutes, until dough sticks together and is easy to work with.

With a rolling pin, roll dough to between ¼" and ½" thickness.

Cut with small cutter and place in a lightly greased baking sheet.

Bake 50 minutes at 325 degrees.

Cool on a rack until hard and store, at room temperature, in a container with a loose-fitting lid.

Plaque Buster Dog Biscuits

This biscuit has a very hard, crunchy texture that will help scrape the build-up of plaque off your dog's teeth. Makes about 70 small biscuits.

Ingredients:

¾ cup powdered skim milk

½ cup cornmeal, stone ground

¼ cup bulgur wheat

2 ¼ cups whole wheat flour

1 chicken bouillon cube

1 ½ cups boiling water

1 cup quick rolled oats

1 egg, beaten

Directions:

In a mixing bowl, combine powdered skim milk, cornmeal, bulgur wheat and flour and set aside.

In a large mixing bowl, dissolve bouillon cube in boiling water.

Add rolled oats and let stand, about 5 minutes. Then stir in beaten egg.

Gradually stir in dry ingredients, half a cup at a time, until well blended. The last few capfuls, blend in with your hands.

Divide dough into 2 balls, so it is easy to work with.

Knead each dough ball on a floured surface, about 5 minutes.

With a rolling pin, roll dough between ¼ to ½ inch thickness.

Cut with cutter and place on baking sheet, lined with foil.

Bake 50 minutes at 325 degrees.

Turn oven off and let biscuits cool several hours or overnight, in the oven.

Store, at room temperature, in a container with a loose-fitting lid.

Weed-Be-Gone

This may seem like an odd thing to have in a recipe but it is a recipe and it works amazingly well.

Instead of the expensive weed killers on the market, use this recipe and see how it works.

I took this recipe off my Facebook page when our friend Cheryl McGraw posted it.

Hank used it and was thrilled at how well it worked!

Ingredients:

1 gallon vinegar

2 cups Epson Salt

¼ cup Dawn Dish Soap (The Blue Original)

Directions:

It will kill anything you spray it on. Just mix and spray in the morning, after the dew has evaporated. Walk away. Go back after dinner and the weeds are gone.

Cheaper than anything you can buy anywhere! Never buy Round-up again!

Index

APPETIZERS

Almost-Famous Spinach-Artichoke Dip 11

Beer-Cheese Triangles with Zesty Cheese Sauce 10

Buttery Mushrooms 16

Crab Rangoon Dip 17

Crisp Crab Cakes 12

Deviled Eggs 4

Five Layer Mexican Dip 14

Fried Mozzarella-Pepperoni Egg Roll 8

Hot Artichoke Spread 9

Hot and Hearty Beef and Bean Dip 6

Hot Cheesy Artichoke & Spinach Dip 19

Hot Crab Dip 13

Louisiana Hot Crab Dip 18

Nachos Supreme 7

Tangy Cheese Ball 5

SALADS AND SOUPS

Best Ever Coleslaw 34

Bobbie's Chili..21

Broccoli Salad 26

Chilistroni 32

Cool Whip Salad...29

Crab Pasta Salad 31

Creamy Avocado Pasta Salad 36

Crockpot French Onion Soup 38

Cucumber Salad in a Jar 33

Egg Drop Soup 24

Healthy Shrimp Salad...35

Oriental Slaw 30

Potato Soup 25

Quick Crab Stew 23

Shrimp and Pineapple Lettuce Cups 37

Spanish Potato Salad...28

Tex-Mex Salad 27

White Chili 22

BREADS AND ROLLS

Banana Bread #1 54

Banana Bread #2 60

Basic Bread for Beginners 58

Beer Bread 53

Buttery Soft Pretzels 49

Griddle Flat Bread 46

Homemade Pan Rolls 51

Monkey Bread 55

Muffins That Taste Like Doughnuts 40

Poppy Seed Bread..48

Red Lobster Cheese Biscuits 47

Simple Flat Bread..43

Southern Biscuits...56

Surprise Muffins..45

Yeast Free Bread..42

ENTREES

Asian Pot Roast with Sweet and Sour Sauce 80

Barbecued Salmon with Fresh Nectarine Salsa 74

Bobbie's Meatballs (Meatloaf) 86

Bobbie's Taco Salad 67

Broiled Salmon with Tomato Cream Sauce for two 70

Carols Easy Crockpot Sauce for over Rice 73

Chicken Pot Pie 85

Chinese Pork Chops 82

Crock Pot Ham and Bean Soup 71

Crock Pot Lasagna 75

Crock Pot Lasagna #2 76

Easy, Tasty Pulled Pork 79

Fish Tacos 77

Grilled Fish in Butter 66

Maple-Brined Pork 83

Maxine's Pork Hangovers 87

Shrimp and Mango Stir-Fry 64

Shrimp Boat Spaghetti 63

West Coast Turkey Burger 68

White Chicken Enchiladas 62

SIDE DISHES

Angel Hair Pasta with Garlic, Herbs and Parm. 96

Baked Beans from Scratch 99

Cheesy Cauliflower Au Gratin..98

Cheesy Cauliflower Patties 104

Creamed Spinach 93

Easy Broccoli & Cheddar Casserole 89

Garlic-Mint Peas 90

Mexican Rice..91

Mom's Scalloped Corn 105

Onion Pie 102

Roasted Asparagus...101

Smashed Potatoes 94

Stovetop Mac n Cheese 103

Tomato Pie 92

Veggie Fries...95

Vegetable Pie 106

DESSERTS

Apple Crisp 129

Brownie Bowl Sundaes 112

Chocolate Éclair Cake 127

Easy Apple Fritters 115

Easy Pineapple Upside Down Cake 117

Funnel Cake 130

Marge's Cherry Cheesecake 108

Maxine's Grape Pie 121

Maxine's Peach Cobbler 122

Maxine's Sugar Cookies 123

Mexican Flan 119

One Bowl Apple Cake 124

Pepsi Cake 125

Pineapple Upside Down Cake in the Slow Cooker 114

Pink Lady 109

Reese's Peanut Putter No Bake Bars 111

Soft Oatmeal Cookies 120

Two Ingredient Lemon Bars 110

Ultimate Blueberry Cake/Coffee Cake 113

BEVERAGES

Beer Margarita **138**

Best Ever Lemonade **136**

Carrot Cake Cocktail **132**

Eggnog **139**

Electric Lemonade **143**

English Channel **140**

Internal Detox for Glowing Skin **134**

Old-School Melon Cocktails **141**

Orange Julius **133**

Peanut Butter-Nana-Strawberry Smoothie **142**

Punch **137**

Southern Sweet Ice Tea **135**

CONDIMENTS

Black Bean Salsa 150

Coney Dog Sauce 152

Creamy Cucumber Salsa 148

Fresh Salsa 145

Fruit Salsa 151

Grilled Pineapple Salsa 147

Honey Soy Marinade 156

Ketchup Variations 154

Lobster Salsa 149

Spicy Garlic Dressing 146

Strawberry Freezer Jam 153

MISC

Bread and Butter Slices 159

Economy Dog Cookies 162

Flea Fighter Fingers Dog Cookies 160

Miracle Granola 158

Plaque Buster Dog Biscuits 163

Weed-Be-Gone 165

ABOUT THE AUTHOR

Bobbie Altschul is a mother, grandmother and great grandmother as well as the author of *Fraser the Christmas Tree*, her first children's book, *Delusional*, a novel and the Gypsy Series novels. The Gypsy Series includes *Gypsy Escape*, *Gypsy Child* and *Gypsy Coins* at this printing. Bobbie is currently working on the fourth of that series.

Made in the USA
Charleston, SC
10 October 2014